RAND

Chronic Juvenile Offenders

Final Results from The Skillman Aftercare Experiment

Peter W. Greenwood, Elizabeth Piper Deschenes,
John Adams

Supported by
The Skillman Foundation

Preface

This document is the final report on a four-year evaluation of two experimental intensive aftercare programs that were designed to help delinquent youth from Detroit and Pittsburgh return to their homes following residential placements. The experimental programs and evaluation effort were supported by generous grants from The Skillman Foundation of Detroit, Michigan.

This report should interest anyone concerned with the design and implementation of effective community-based supervision programs for serious delinquents.

Contents

Tables

Summary

Background

Every year, thousands of delinquent youth who have been removed from their homes and placed in residential programs, because of the seriousness or frequency of their criminal behavior, are released right back into the same communities and home situations in which their delinquent behavior developed and flourished, often without any coordinated attempt to ensure that their old patterns of delinquency and dysfunctional behavior are not reestablished. And, in fact, many of these youth do fall back into their old ways and end up in another juvenile or adult correctional facility. This cycle of inadequate aftercare and recidivism occurs in spite of the fact that many criminologists and correctional practitioners have long articulated their belief that the failure rate for these youth could be substantially reduced by providing them with appropriate amounts of aftercare supervision and services. The most prominent reasons for this belief include the lack of other supportive community resources and the dysfunctional environment to which many youth are returned.

Methods

The Skillman Intensive Aftercare Program Initiative was designed to test and determine the value of intensive aftercare supervision and services for high-risk delinquents. Under this initiative, two experimental programs, embodying common core features, were established in Detroit, Michigan, and Pittsburgh, Pennsylvania. Eligible youth, who were being returned from residential placements to homes in these sites, were randomly assigned to either the new program conditions or the regular forms of post-release supervision used in their community. In each site, the experimental programs were developed and run by experienced private providers.

Youth assigned to the experimental programs were supposed to be released from their residential placement two months early and to receive the intensive aftercare supervision for the next six months. Other key components of the experimental program included: pre-release contacts and planning between the assigned aftercare worker, the youth, and his family; an intensive level of supervision and counseling involving several contacts a day; efforts to resolve family problems and improve functioning; efforts to mobilize and involve youth with appropriate community services and programs; and highly motivated and energetic caseworkers. The program model upon which the experimental programs were based had been used extensively in Massachusetts with supposedly good results.

Data for assessing the characteristics of participating youths, and the content and effect of the programs, were obtained by: coding background data from agency records; interviewing caseworkers during each youth's six-month program; interviewing youth just before and one year following their release to the community; and coding arrest records for the follow-up period.

Implementation

Approximately 100 youth were randomly assigned to the experimental and control conditions in each site during the period of the evaluation. In both sites, the experimental programs were implemented more or less as planned. In both sites, youth assigned to the experimental programs received considerably more pre-release contacts and post-release supervision and services than the controls. However, there were differences between the two programs in the timing of each youth's release, in their intensity of supervision, and in the sanctions they could impose.

The Pittsburgh youth were released from their residential placements two months early, as had been originally planned, whereas the Detroit youth did not get any time cut from their residential terms. The Pittsburgh program reintegrated youth from residential programs run by its parent agency, whereas the Detroit program had the more difficult task of coordinating with state training school staff. In the Pittsburgh program, caseworkers made sure that they saw their youth several times a day; in the Detroit program, less than one contact per day was averaged. The Pittsburgh program was also authorized to temporarily return youth to their residential facility for failing to abide by program guidelines; the program in Detroit had no such powers. Finally, the Pittsburgh youth had more extensive records than those from Detroit in terms of their prior arrests and placements, making them a greater risk for future criminal involvement.

Outcomes

Differences in program content appeared to have had little or no effect on the final outcomes. In neither site did the experimental program appear to have a significant effect on the behavior of participating youth. In neither site did we find significant differences between experimental and control groups in the proportion of youth arrested or self-reporting offenses or drug use during the 12 month follow-up period. Nor did the experimental programs appear to have any effect on the involvement of youth in work or school, in spite of the effort devoted by the aftercare caseworkers to establishing contacts in these areas. There was some evidence of positive effects of the experimental programs on youth's personal goals, sense of self-efficacy, and coping skills, but these effects were not consistent and did not appear to be associated with behavioral outcomes.

Discussion

A number of factors might account for the fact that our evaluation failed to detect any significant differences in behavior between the experimental and control samples. One is the limited size of the samples. The smaller the sample, the lower the probability that an experiment will detect any given difference in effects. In either site, with a sample of approximately 50 experimental and 50 control youth, the probability of detecting a relative 20 percent change in a base recidivism rate of 50 percent is only 0.26. The probability of detecting a relative 20 percent change from a base rate of 20 percent is only 0.13. With a larger sample, some of the differences found in this study might have approached the significance level.

It may be that the aftercare workers were ineffective in assessing the progress or needs of individual youth or in assisting them in getting the kinds of services they needed. However, the solid reputations of the provider agencies and our own observations suggest that the quality of services provided was consistent with those usually encountered in this field. A more likely reason for our failure to detect significant improvements in the post-release behavior of youth participating in the experimental programs is that the surveillance/casework approach is simply inappropriate or inadequate for dealing with the kinds of situations these young men face.

The cost-effectiveness of intensive aftercare programming, and appropriate strategies for improving it, appear to depend on the amount of criminality demonstrated by the youth such programs are meant to serve or control. For relatively low-risk youth, such as those found in our Detroit sample, intensive aftercare may be a cost-effective substitute for time in residential placement, even if it does not improve the behavior of participating youth, who appear to represent a risk of less than one felony crime per year following their release from custody.

For more serious youth offenders, such as those in our Pittsburgh sample, it appears that a prompt custodial response to subsequent arrests or violations of program conditions may do more to protect the public than the kinds of efforts devoted to improving access to schooling or jobs that were tested here. Half the arrests experienced by the experimental group in Pittsburgh were preceded by at least one other arrest during the follow-up period.

In any case, the levels of intensive aftercare supervision and services for chronic juvenile offenders, as provided in this demonstration project, appear to have had much less effect on subsequent behavior than many of the advocates of aftercare or intensive supervision had hoped. Future attempts to reduce post-release recidivism should probably devote more attention to programming that addresses risk factors more directly related to delinquent behavior, such as substance abuse treatment and anger management.

Acknowledgments

We gratefully acknowledge The Skillman Foundation, its director, Leonard W. Smith, and our grant monitors, John Ziraldo, Kari Schlachtenhaufen, and Lisa Kaichen for their generous funding and support of this project. We wish to thank the staff of Diversified Youth Services in Michigan and VisionQuest in Pennsylvania for providing the services to the youth in the study. We are also grateful to the Wayne County Department of Social Services and the Adult Recorders' Court in Michigan and the Allegheny County Juvenile and Adult Courts in Pittsburgh for their cooperation in implementing the experimental programs and in collecting these data.

We would also like to acknowledge the assistance of RAND staff, including Susan Turner, Kathy Rosenblatt, Andrea Wiideman, Grant Marshall, Milinda Cush, Helen Giglio, Mary Sauters, Carolyn Kono, and our many interviewers and coders, particularly Barbara Kuykindall and Wendy Savage in Detroit and Joe Fasekas and Paula McCommons in Pittsburgh. Finally, we would like to thank the young people in Detroit and Pittsburgh for their cooperation in this research project.

1. Introduction

Every year, thousands of youth, primarily males between the ages of 13 and 17, are placed in residential facilities by juvenile courts because of their repeated or serious criminal activities. Longitudinal studies show that before these placements, most of these youth have developed patterns of antisocial and dysfunctional behavior which include lack of self-control; early experimentation with tobacco, alcohol, illicit drugs, and sex; lack of commitment to education and poor performance in school; and many previous arrests (Elliott et al., 1989; Farrington, 1990; Huizinga, et al., 1991; Gottfredson and Hirschi, 1990). Many criminologists agree that inadequate, inappropriate, or inconsistent parental supervision is an important factor associated with all of these problem behaviors. In most states, each juvenile placed in a residential program costs somewhere between $30,000 to $40,000 per year (Thornberry et al., 1989). During the time they are in residential placements, most of these youth will show substantial gains in scholastic achievement and social functioning while participating in a variety of educational, rehabilitative, and recreational programs. In many of these programs, youth have an opportunity to work their way through several phases, with each successive step earning them increased responsibilities and privileges.

Unfortunately, for many of these youth, the gains in prosocial behavior and scholastic involvement are not maintained when they return to their homes and communities. Instead, many fall back into their old networks of friends and patterns of behavior and are soon back in court on new criminal charges (Greenwood and Zimring, 1985).

There are a number of reasons to believe that the usual practice of investing all of the resources devoted to a delinquent youth's treatment in residential programs, without spending a significant amount on reintegrating the youth back into the community, may not be wise (Altschuler and Armstrong, 1991). Common sense tells us that most individuals are likely to experience problems in moving from a highly structured and supportive environment, such as that maintained in most residential programs, to one that is much more chaotic and stressful. Furthermore, given the state of most school systems in the impoverished communities where most of these youth are likely to live, and the youth's prior record of poor performance, many can be expected to face problems finding and enrolling in appropriate educational programs. And, with the high unemployment rates typically found in their communities, many of them can be expected to face problems finding any, let alone meaningful, work.

In addition to these practical issues, follow-up studies show that when these youth return home they are likely to be back in contact with many of the factors that contributed to their delinquent behavior: delinquent and/or drug-using peers; dysfunctional parents or households; and an excess of illegitimate opportunities (primarily drug selling and auto theft) compared to legitimate employment (Greenwood and Turner, 1993). All these risk factors increase the likelihood that youth will return to their involvement in crime.

There are a number of theoretical reasons to believe that appropriate aftercare services can improve a youth's chances for successful reintegration. Strain theorists have argued that delinquency is caused by lower-class youth's frustrations in their inability to achieve normal aspirations through legitimate means (Merton, 1968; Cloward and Ohlin, 1960). Aftercare services can help these youth achieve appropriate employment. Control theorists argue that delinquency is more likely when a youth is not sufficiently involved with conventional community institutions, such as his family, school, or church (Hirschi, 1969). An effective aftercare program can attempt to facilitate such involvements.

Finally, social learning theorists argue that delinquent behavior is shaped through the sequence of rewards and punishments encountered in everyday life (Akers, 1977). An aftercare program can attempt to monitor a youth's behavior and provide appropriate rewards and sanctions in response to the behavior that is observed. The aftercare worker can also serve as a role model for appropriate behavior in situations similar to those a youth might encounter.

In recent years, many corrections officials have become more attuned to the need for some type of transitional aftercare services (Altschuler and Armstrong, 1991). However, few have been successful in finding the funds to put such efforts into place, as most states continue to struggle just to keep up with their steadily growing prison populations. In most states it appears that the immediate and more certain public safety benefits of incapacitation continue to outweigh the more speculative and long-term benefits of reduced recidivism that effective aftercare programs might provide.

Only a few states support significant aftercare or transitional services and these have never been effectively evaluated (Ohlin et al., 1978; Fagan, 1990). This report describes the results of an experiment designed to assess the effects of intensive aftercare supervision and services on the behavior of chronic juvenile offenders. The project began with an invitation from The Skillman Foundation to develop and test a program that might improve the quality of correctional services available to delinquent youth from the Detroit area. After an initial pilot study to identify gaps in existing programs and to judge the receptivity of public officials to various program options, it was determined that the most productive course of action would be to test an intensive aftercare program that would embody what were thought to be the most effective methods of supervision and support known to the field.

With generous support from The Skillman Foundation, private providers in two sites, Detroit and Pittsburgh,[1] were selected to implement a model that had been developed in Massachusetts and used there successfully for more than 15 years. Key elements of the model included: planning of post-release activities while youth are still in custody; frequent supervisory contacts with the youth (several times a day) after their release; supervision by well-trained caseworkers who are both friendly and supportive but firm in insisting on appropriate behavior; efforts to improve family functioning and relations between the youth and other family members; and assistance for the youth in obtaining appropriate educational or vocational placements.

Over a period of two years, about 100 youth completing residential placements in each site were randomly assigned to receive either the experimental intensive aftercare or regular supervision. Information about the youth and their subsequent behavior was obtained through two rounds of interviews with the youth themselves, interviews with their caseworkers, and coding of criminal justice case files and records.

Although the experimental programs may have had some success in modifying the youth's values and beliefs in a positive direction, it does not appear that they resulted in substantial changes in post-release behavior or likelihood of arrest.

The next section of this report describes the experimental aftercare programs and our research design. Subsequent sections present the results of our implementation and outcome evaluations, respectively. The final section discusses the implications of this study for aftercare policy and future research.

---

[1]Diversified Youth Services (DYS) operated the program in Detroit. The VisionQuest (VQ) program in Pittsburgh was referred to as HomeQuest.

2. Research Design and Methods

Subjects

The experimental aftercare intervention was applied to two samples of male delinquents who were returning to their homes after successfully completing placements in residential correctional programs. One of the samples consisted of youth returning to families in the Detroit area from a training school run by the Michigan Department of Social Services (DSS).[1] The other sample consisted of youth returning to homes in the Pittsburgh area after completing a placement with VisionQuest (VQ), a private provider that receives many of the more serious youth offenders placed by the Allegheny County Juvenile Court and uses wilderness camps and wagon trains as settings for program activities (Greenwood and Turner, 1987b). Eligibility in both sites was limited to youth who were returning to live with their families and initially included youth from anywhere in the county.[2] However, after discovering how long it took workers to get out and contact youth in outlying areas, both programs limited eligibility to youth from the city.

The Detroit youth were predominantly black males (89 percent) and averaged 17 years of age. They were likely to be living in female-headed households, where income was provided by public assistance. On the average, they had completed only 8 grades and over 40 percent had a learning or emotional disability. The majority (82 percent) had also been a discipline problem in school. The average age at first arrest was 14.4 years and they averaged three prior arrests. Less than one-third were known as gang members, but over half of them were known to be drug dealers. Their records indicated that almost 50 percent of them had been using alcohol or drugs (see Table A.1 for a more detailed breakdown).

The VisionQuest program is used by the Allegheny County Juvenile Court for the more chronic delinquents who have often failed in other placements. As might be expected, these youth were somewhat more serious offenders than

---

[1]The state-run training schools are the primary residential placements for medium- and high-level-custody youth adjudicated delinquents and committed as wards of the state in Michigan.

[2]In practice, very few youth were excluded on the basis of this criterion of placement in the family. However, since this decision was made before the call to RAND for random assignment, the exact number excluded is unknown. At least one youth in the Detroit program was supervised even though he was living in a group home setting.

those in residential placement in Detroit. The Pittsburgh sample also constituted predominantly black males from female-headed households where only one-third of the income was from employment. On average, the youth had completed the 9th grade, and most had been a discipline problem or showed some learning disability. The average ages at first arrest and adjudication were slightly younger for this group, compared to the sample in Detroit, yet they were older at current placement. The Pittsburgh youth had, on average, five prior arrests and four adjudications, with two prior placements. Although they appear to be chronic offenders more than youth in Detroit, their current offense was more likely to be a property one. Few were known gang members or drug dealers, but almost half were known to have a drug problem (see Table A.2 for a more detailed breakdown).

Youth from the two sites also differed in their pattern of self-reported offending and drug use (see Tables A.3 and A.4). Over 85 percent of the Detroit youth reported having committed a felony assault. Over 85 percent also reported having used alcohol or marijuana in the past year; 6 percent reported using cocaine and 9 percent reported using crack. The Pittsburgh youth were less likely to report having committed crimes against persons (just over 50 percent reported felony assault) and more likely to report property crimes (90 percent reported a felony theft). Almost all of the youth reported use of alcohol or marijuana, about 28 percent had used cocaine, and only 6 percent reported use of crack. In general, the Pittsburgh youth appear to have been more chronic delinquents and more involved with drugs than those in Detroit training schools.

Random Assignment and Follow-Up Procedures

In both Detroit and Pittsburgh, youth were identified as eligible for the intensive aftercare program by staff in the residential programs. In Detroit, most of the youth were referred by group leaders at the Maxey or Adrian Training Schools[3] approximately three months before their release. As names were called in to RAND for the random assignment, they would be assigned to the control or experimental group. For the latter, the aftercare program worker would be notified immediately so that pre-release planning could begin.

In Pittsburgh, youth referred to VisionQuest from the Allegheny County Juvenile Court had more determinate release dates. Youth were referred to the experiment by VisionQuest East Coast treatment workers three months before

---

[3]The majority of the youth (90 percent) were referred from Maxey; only 10 youth were referred from Adrian.

their expected date of release. Youth who were assigned to the experimental group would be transferred from their current impact program[4] to the transitional group home at the Franklin wilderness camp for a one-month period to prepare for release to their families. Youth in the control group would remain on the wagon train and might return for a short time to the wilderness camp before their court release hearing.

As soon as youth had been assigned to the experimental or control program, RAND on-site field staff began data collection. Youth were asked if they would agree to participate in the study. Background information was collected from program files and youth participated in an intake interview that lasted approximately 45 minutes, for which they were paid $10. Very few youth refused to participate in the evaluation at either site (two in Detroit and four in Pittsburgh). Each youth who agreed to participate was asked to provide information for future contact (several relatives and friends) and was informed that an interview would be conducted approximately 12 months following his release to the community. The address of their parents was also collected from the background files at the training school or residential placement. The one-year follow-up procedures consisted of attempting to contact the youth at his last known address or attempting to locate him through the other contacts he had listed or through information provided by the caseworker.

The Intervention

The basic assumption underlying the experimental intervention was that intensive supervision and assistance by well-trained aftercare workers would increase the likelihood of youth becoming involved in prosocial activities; decrease their likelihood of becoming involved with delinquent peers; and provide opportunities to address minor slips in behavior, without waiting until the youth became involved in more serious criminal activity.

The program selected as a model for the experimental intervention was the "tracking" program operated by The Key Programs, Inc., in various localities in Massachusetts. Officials and staff from the two experimental program providers participated in a three-day training session run by Key, as part of the process of designing their programs.

---

[4]VisionQuest youth must successfully complete three "impact programs" that include wilderness camps, wagon trains, tall ships, bicycle touring, and other "outward bound" type activities (Greenwood and Turner, 1987b).

The basic components of the tracking model included:

1. *Prerelease contacts and planning between the assigned aftercare caseworker, the youth, and his family.*

The primary goals of this activity are for the parties to become acquainted with each other; the youth to become familiar with what will be expected of him; and the caseworker to begin assessing the situation and developing a plan. The prerelease contact period usually will involve several visits by the youth to his home, accompanied by his caseworker.

2. *An intensive level of supervision involving several contacts a day.*

One goal of the program is to ensure that the youth follow a carefully prescribed program during the first few weeks after their release. The degree of control exercised by the caseworker is gradually reduced then and turned over to the parents. The purpose of the visits is to keep track of each youth's activities and whereabouts; assess how well the youth is doing; and provide appropriate assistance, counseling, and feedback.

3. *Efforts to improve family functioning and supervision of the youth.*

Many delinquent youth come from families that do not function well (Loeber and Loeber, 1986; Farrington, 1990). The goal of this component is to assist the families in becoming a more stabilizing force in the lives of their children, through counseling, friendship, and linkages with other family resources. Although some of the families seemed to appreciate and benefit from these efforts, many did not care to become involved.

4. *Efforts to mobilize and involve youth with appropriate social services or work.*

Much of the caseworkers' efforts went into helping youth locate and enroll in appropriate educational programs or jobs. The caseworkers quickly developed familiarity with supportive resources in their areas and attempted to work with each youth to meet his needs. This task proved particularly frustrating in that the youth had a tendency to drop out when these positions did not live up to their expectations.

5. *Highly motivated and energetic caseworkers.*

One assumption of the tracking model is that the youth will copy behavior that is modeled by his caseworker, if there is some positive identification. The caseworker was expected to maintain friendly and cordial relations with the youth and his parents, yet to be firm in his or her intolerance of inappropriate behavior.

Although there were considerable differences in how the two private providers implemented the experimental program in their respective sites, both programs made serious efforts to incorporate all the components of the Key model.

In both sites, youth were supervised by teams of two or three caseworkers, most of whom were young adult males. All the caseworkers in Detroit were black, as were about half in Pittsburgh. In both sites, caseworkers routinely established contacts with youth and their families to begin the pre-release planning process. In both sites, caseworkers spent most of their time tracking the youth, interacting with them and their families, and attempting to get them involved in educational programs or jobs.

Most of their interactions with the youth could be characterized as relaxed and informal. Several of the families invited caseworkers to important family functions. In both sites, the caseworkers used a variety of strategies to help youth and their families understand the risk and dangers of substance and alcohol abuse. Many of the families participated in developing genograms[5] that helped identify dysfunctional family members.

The Detroit program was directed by a clinical psychologist who favored what he characterized as a humanistic approach to the youth and his family, attempting to work with them on problems and issues that they believed to be important. One result of this approach was that contacts tended to be longer but less frequent than those in Pittsburgh. The Pittsburgh program was directed and staffed by individuals who had worked in other components of VQ's extensive array of programs and took a more directed and control-oriented approach than the program in Detroit.

The two programs differed in their initial release procedures and in their ability to impose sanctions on youth for negative behavior. About one month before their planned release date, the Pittsburgh youth were moved from the VQ wagon train to a transitional group home outside Pittsburgh. From there, they made home visits and then moved back into their homes. The Detroit youth were moved directly from the training schools to their homes. The VQ staff were permitted to return youth to the group home or wilderness programs for short periods, in response to inappropriate behavior. The Detroit program had no such power.

In both sites, control youth in the group received minimal attention and services from their regularly assigned caseworkers (DSS community caseworkers in

---

[5]Genograms are diagrams of family relationships which can be used to trace inherited characteristics such as alcoholism.

Detroit and Allegheny County probation officers in Pittsburgh) other than brief meetings several times a month, frequently in the caseworker's office. A few of the control youth in Pittsburgh were placed on intensive probation supervision.

Data-Collection and Assessment Procedures

The evaluation incorporated both process and outcome components in a classic experimental design. Eligible youth were randomly assigned to experimental and control conditions by the evaluators. Information on key background and outcome measures was collected through personal interviews and the coding of official records immediately after assignment and one year following release to the community. Various measures of program intensity and character were collected through personal interviews with the youth and their caseworkers.

A Background Assessment Form was used to code information from each youth's case records regarding: personal and family characteristics; record of prior arrests and placements; educational achievement; health; problem behaviors; emotional problems; gang involvement; and any record of substance abuse or familial abuse or neglect.

Baseline interviews with participating youth were scheduled immediately after random assignment before release from the residential facility. In addition to completing a calendar detailing their place of residence and status for the three years preceding their current placement (see Appendix B for a complete listing of all the variables included), these interviews provided information on: self-reported delinquency and drug use during the year preceding their placement (using a slightly modified version of the measures used by Elliott et al. (1989) for the National Youth Survey); exposure to delinquent peers; personal goals; self-efficacy; and coping skills for dealing with a variety of high-risk situations (these items are described more fully in Section 4).

Most of the items on the baseline pre-release interviews were also included in the 12-month follow-up interviews. These follow-up interviews also included: youth's perceptions of the aftercare program and their primary aftercare caseworker; and their experiences with their families, jobs, and school.

Information regarding the frequency of contacts and other services provided to the youth was obtained through two interviews with assigned caseworkers, three months and six months following the youth's return to the community.

Follow-up information on arrests and convictions was obtained by coding: DSS and Adult Recorders' Court records in Wayne County (Michigan); and juvenile and adult probation records in Pittsburgh. The adult records include only those arrests that were brought to court, not those that resulted in release by the police or a refusal to prosecute by the District Attorney.

Sample Attrition and Response Bias

To increase response rates and prevent study attrition, we had planned initially for monthly telephone contacts with youth to verify their addresses and ask them how they were doing. In addition, we had planned to conduct interviews at three months and six months post-release to obtain more recent and accurate information on their activities. However, we found it difficult and costly in terms of time and expenses to maintain contact with these youth over an extended period of time. Most of the three- and six-month interviews were postponed and administered at the 12-month follow-up.

We experienced most of our problems with sample attrition during the third and fourth years of the study. Because of a gap in our funding, we were forced to postpone pre-release interviews in Pittsburgh for the last group of subjects assigned to the study; we also had to postpone the 12-month follow-up interviews for a period of six months until we could hire new interviewers in both sites. Because of these delays, we lost contact with some of our subjects and with their caseworkers who might have been able to provide addresses or telephone numbers. The consequences of this discontinuity in funding on the response rate for the interviews are shown in the Table 2.1. In Detroit, we

Table 2.1

Number of Completed Forms and Youth Interviews by Site and Condition

	Control	Experimental	Total
Detroit (n=100)			
Background	47	50	97
Pre-release	47	49	96
Pre-release (delayed)	0	0	0
Three- and six-month follow-up	12	18	30
12-month follow-up	22	29	51
Pre-release and follow-up	22	29	51
Pittsburgh (n=87)			
Background	40	46	86
Pre-release	24	41	65
Pre-release (delayed)	12	5	17
Three- and six-month follow-up[a]	34	37	71
12-month follow-up	35	38	73
Pre-release and follow-up	23	33	56

[a]Includes only those who also had a 12-month follow-up.

succeeded in collecting follow-up interviews with only 52 percent of the initial sample. In Pittsburgh, the follow-up response rate was a more respectable 85 percent, but because of the delayed pre-release interviews, we have both pre-release and follow-up data for only 65 percent, which includes a much higher percentage of experimentals than controls.

Given the differential response rates in the two sites for the pre-release and follow-up interviews, several analyses were conducted to examine possible attrition bias. Using earlier research on risk and recidivism prediction (Greenwood and Abrahamse, 1982; Gottfredson, 1987), we selected six background variables on which to compare the interviewed and noninterviewed subjects by condition: race, prior drug use, type of current offense, age at first arrest, number of prior arrests, and age at current placement. The samples were compared across condition and interview status over time, using chi-square tests of association for the categorical variables and t-tests for the continuous variables. Although there were no differences resulting from the random assignment of youth to the experimental and control conditions, we did find some significant differences between the samples who had the pre-release and/or follow-up interviews. These differences are shown in Table A.5 for Detroit and Table A.6 for Pittsburgh.

For Detroit, there are only two sample sizes, one for the background data (n=97) and one for the follow-up interview (n=51).[6] As shown in Table A.5, we found only one significant difference for the youth in Detroit. Those who were interviewed were more likely to have committed crimes against persons than those who were not interviewed. Because the attrition does not vary by condition,[7] the analysis sample for the outcome data was not weighted.

Because of the complications in collecting the Pittsburgh data, there are four different sample sizes. Of the 86 youth for whom we collected background data, we had complete pre-release interviews for 65 and incomplete data for 17. Complete follow-up information was available for 73 of them (85 percent of the sample). Since 17 of the 73 youth interviewed at follow-up had no data for some of the variables on the pre-release interview, the comparison of pre-release and follow-up data is based on the sample of 56 youths (65 percent) who had complete information for the pre-release and follow-up interviews. For each subsample (n=65, 73, 56), we compared the control and experimental groups on

---

[6]One youth did not have a pre-release interview, but this was too small a sample size for calculations of differences.

[7]In addition, the bias does not favor the experimental group.

the same six variables as in the analysis of the Detroit data. We also compared those interviewed to those not interviewed, controlling for condition.

As shown in Table A.6, we found no differences by either condition or interview status for the 65 youth with complete pre-release interviews. However, there were two significant differences for those interviewed (n=73) in comparison to those not interviewed at follow-up. Among those in the experimental group, those who were not interviewed were much more likely than those who were interviewed to have a drug use problem. Youth in the control group who were older at the time of placement were less likely to be interviewed than those who were younger at intake. These same differences between the interviewed and noninterviewed youth (in percentage of drug users and age at current placement) were found for the reduced sample of 56 youth with both pre-release and follow-up interviews. Therefore, we attempted to correct for the attrition bias.

Logistic regression analysis was used to model the probability of being interviewed at pre-release and follow-up and to derive weights to control for possible interview bias in the Pittsburgh sample. The same variables selected previously to test for differences between the interviewed and noninterviewed groups were entered into a stepwise logistic regression model. This procedure was used for both the sample of 73 with follow-up interviews and the sample of 56 with both pre-release and follow-up interviews (in comparison to the sample of 86 with background data). We were unable to find a good fit for the data for those with only follow-up interviews (n=73); all of the variables dropped out of the analysis because they did not meet the criterion for inclusion in the model. For the sample of 56 with both pre-release and follow-up interviews, several variables were significant in predicting the interview status, including the percentage of youth with drug use problems, age at first arrest, age at current placement, and the interaction effects of age at first arrest by condition and problem drug use by condition. Using the parameters from this model, we derived weights for the sample of 56 to be used in the analyses of the changes in personal goals, coping skills, self-esteem, and friends' behavior.

3. Implementation

One critical issue in evaluating the effect of any experimental intervention involves assessing the character and strength of the intervention itself and determining in what ways the treatment of the experimental and control subjects differs. This section presents and discusses a number of measures that can be used to assess the content, intensity, and quality of aftercare services and supervision provided to the various experimental groups. The first issue addressed is the amount of time youth served in their residential placements, and the extent to which the experimental youth were released earlier than the others. Next, we describe the frequency and nature of contacts by the aftercare workers, followed by the youth's perceptions of the aftercare program and their particular caseworker. The last item covered is the relative costs of the programs.

Time Served and Early Release

We have previously alluded to the fact that the original goal of the experimental program was to substitute six months of intensive aftercare for the last two months of residential placement. However, because the Michigan Training School staff did not modify the normal peer review process, the experimental youth in Michigan were not released early. In fact, the average time served in residential placement by the experimental youth in Detroit (17.1 months) was slightly longer than the average for the controls (16.9 months). In Pittsburgh, VisionQuest and the Juvenile Court ensured that the experimental youth served exactly two months less than the controls (10.2 compared to 12.1 months).

Frequency and Nature of Contacts

One goal of the experimental programs was to have the caseworkers stay in frequent contact with the youth, particularly during the first few months after their release, so that they could closely monitor their behavior and provide counseling or assistance to them or their families in a timely manner.

Information regarding the frequency of contacts was obtained through interviews with caseworkers and youth at three and six months.[1]

Tables 3.1 and 3.2 present average monthly rates for specific types of contacts based on these two different sources. Although there are some differences between them,[2] they basically tell the same story. The frequency of contact achieved by the experimental programs was several orders of magnitude greater than that experienced by the controls. According to caseworkers in Detroit, the experimental program averaged about 10 face-to-face contacts per month over the six months of the program, compared to one or two such contacts for the controls. For both groups, contacts were more frequent during the first two months and then gradually tapered off. The Pittsburgh experimental program averaged 60 face-to-face contacts per month over the six months of the program compared to about five such contacts per month for the controls. There were also differences in the nature of these contacts. Aftercare workers in both

Table 3.1

Program Implementation: Monthly Rates from Youth Interviews

	Detroit	
	Control (n=12)	Experimental (n=18)
Months in program	6.8	5.8
Face-to-face contacts	2.3	12.2*
Telephone contacts	6.4	17.4*
Counseling sessions	3.1	6.4
	Pittsburgh	
	Control (n=34)	Experimental (n=37)
Months in program	4.4	5.2
Face-to-face contacts	4.3	42.1*
Telephone contacts	4.0	56.7*
Counseling sessions	2.2	7.2

*Indicates differences that are statistically significant at the 0.05 level, with a two-tailed test.

---

[1]Both caseworkers and youth were asked to estimate the frequency of contacts. Caseworkers were asked to review the daily logs in their files before the interview, but youth did not have this recall aid. Thus, there is some variation in the data reported by the two groups.

[2]We compared the data for those cases for which both youth and caseworker interviews had been completed using correlations and scatterplots. We generally found more agreement in the experimental cases than in the control cases. For the Detroit sample, there were higher correlations between the variables measuring contacts, days in school, and days on the job than for the Pittsburgh sample. We also found very little consistency between caseworkers and youths in the number of counseling sessions attended. This is probably due to different interpretations of the term counseling.

Table 3.2

**Program Implementation: Monthly Rates from
Caseworker Interviews**

	Detroit	
	Control (n=35)	Experimental (n=45)
Months in program	5.2	5.3
Face-to-face contacts	1.5	9.7*
Telephone contacts	3.3	10.4*
Counseling sessions	8.5	7.9
Collateral contacts	1.8	5.7*
	Pittsburgh	
	Control (n=14)	Experimental (n=38)
Months in program	4.9	4.2
Face-to-face contacts	5.3	60.4*
Telephone contacts	3.5	60.2*
Counseling sessions	1.1	16.7*
Collateral contacts	4.6	56.2*

*Indicates differences that are statistically significant
at the 0.05 level, with a two-tailed test.

sites reported that the majority of the face-to-face visits were in the youth's
homes during afternoon or evening hours. In comparison, DSS workers and
probation officers were more likely to visit youth during the day, or see them in
their office. Aftercare workers in Detroit reported that they often spent an hour
or more per visit counseling the youth, whereas VisionQuest workers made more
frequent five- to ten-minute checks and fewer extended contacts.

In addition to the face-to-face contacts that came about as a result of the
caseworkers checking up on the youth, there were also frequent telephone
contacts, initiated by either the caseworker or the youth. The caseworker might
be calling to check up on the youth or provide him with information. The youth
might call the caseworker for advice or assistance, or to inform him where he was
going. In this category, both experimental programs made considerably more
contacts per month than the controls.

Both of the experimental programs scheduled formal individual, family, or peer
group counseling sessions in addition to informal counseling during the face-to-
face home visits.[3] According to the caseworkers, the Detroit experimental

---

[3]The data reported show both informal and formal counseling as defined by the person being
interviewed.

program averaged about eight such sessions per month for each youth, which was no different than the rate reported for the controls.[4] The Pittsburgh program averaged more than 16 such sessions per month (for each youth) compared to only about one per month for the controls.

Judging from just the face-to-face and telephone contacts alone, we find that the Detroit experimental program averaged more than 20 contacts a month compared to fewer than five contacts received by the controls. The primary difference in the nature of these contacts was that the experimental program contacts were much more likely to be unannounced and in the evenings. The Pittsburgh experimental program averaged more than 100 contacts a month (more than three per day) compared to only nine contacts per month for the controls, plus another 56 collateral contacts with family members, friends, teachers, or employers. With this frequency of contact, the Pittsburgh experimental program had fairly detailed knowledge about the location and activity of their youth, except during the late evening hours when it proved difficult or imprudent for the caseworkers to enter some of the projects in which the youth lived, because of drug-trafficking activities.

Youth Perceptions Regarding the Program

The data on frequency of contacts just presented demonstrate that the experimental youth received considerably more attention from their aftercare workers than did the controls, particularly in Pittsburgh. Clearly, the experimental youth were more closely supervised. The next question we would like to have answered is whether the experimental programs provided useful and constructive services to the youth and their families during these contacts, in addition to monitoring their status.

In the absence of any standardized program services whose delivery could be measured, the perceptions of the youth provide a useful way to assess the value of the services. In the follow-up interviews, youth were asked to indicate the degree to which their aftercare or routine supervision program had helped in 11 different domains (see Table A.7 for a listing of the items). In both sites, youth in the experimental programs were considerably more favorable to their aftercare programs than were the controls.

---

[4]Some of the control youth received additional counseling when they were placed in community-based facilities.

In both sites, there were significant differences between the two groups in the overall scale scores on the programs as shown in Table 3.3. Youth in the experimental group in both Detroit and Pittsburgh felt that the aftercare experience helped them reenter the community and helped them better understand themselves and their problems (see Table A.7). Youth in the HomeQuest program were also more likely than those in the control group to report that they got along with their workers and felt the staff really cared about them.

As shown in Table 3.3, the youth ratings of their primary aftercare worker[5] also showed a significant difference between the control and experimental programs in both sites. Youth in the DYS program in Detroit were more likely than those in the control group to feel that their worker was someone who knew them well and with whom they could talk (see Table A.8). The differences between the ratings of the staff in the control and experimental groups in Pittsburgh were significant on almost all the items in the scale, with the exception of feeling they were being checked up on all the time and helping the youth get a job (see Table A.8).

Table 3.3

**Youth Ratings of Aftercare Program and Staff
by Site and Condition**

	Detroit	
	Control (n=19)	Experimental (n=29)
Program	2.6	1.9*
Staff	1.8	1.6
Primary worker	3.0	2.4*

	Pittsburgh	
	Control (n=25)	Experimental (n=36)
Program	3.2	2.4*
Staff	2.6	1.6*
Primary worker	3.4	2.2*

NOTE: A scale score of 1 denotes a positive perception of the program or staff and a scale score of 5 denotes a negative perception.

*Significant difference (p < .05) between control and experimental groups using t-tests.

---

[5]In both sites, youth in the experimental programs had a primary aftercare worker, but they would also have contacts with other workers in the program because staff would rotate days off. In addition, in the Detroit program a family therapist and psychologist worked with the youth. The HomeQuest staff included the workers in the transition group home, the psychologist, and the treatment workers, as well as other trackers.

Costs

The experimental programs were initially designed so that they would not raise the total cost of each youth's placement. At the time that they were implemented, the average daily cost for placements in Michigan Training Schools was about $150 per youth per day and $104 per day in VisionQuest. Our contracts with the private providers agreed to pay $20 per youth per day for aftercare.[6] If youth were released at least one month early from their residential placements, this would save approximately ($104 × 30) $3,120 in Pittsburgh and ($150 × 30) $4,500 in Detroit. If they were placed in aftercare for six months, this would cost ($20 × 6 × 30) $3,600. The savings in residential treatment could more than offset the costs of the aftercare. However, this was not how things turned out.

As we showed above, the experimental youth in Detroit were not released early. It also turned out that neither of the private providers was able to provide the intensity of services that we requested for only $20 per day. VisionQuest negotiated a per diem rate for aftercare services of $33 per day with Allegheny County Probation, counting our $20 a day as a subsidy, so the county only had to pay $13. The Detroit provider required a $94,020 supplement from DSS to finish supervising the last group of youth, bringing their costs up to around $38 per day. Since there were no savings in residential placement costs in Detroit, the aftercare programs resulted in an overall increase in costs per placement, from approximately $76,500 ($150 × 30 × 17) to $82,030 ($76,500 + $276,520/50). In Pittsburgh, the reduced time in residential placement resulted in a slight reduction in total placement costs, from $37,440 ($104 × 30 × 12) without aftercare to $37,140 (($104 × 30 × 10) + ($33 × 30 × 16)) with it.

---

[6]The Detroit program received the total amount allocated for all 50 youth in monthly installments. The Pittsburgh program was paid on a per diem basis for each youth currently receiving services in the program. These differences in the methods of payment resulted in a lower total payment than originally allocated for the Pittsburgh program, since they served fewer than 50 youth and did not incur charges when a youth was AWOL or returned to the criminal justice system.

4. Outcomes

The primary objective of the experimental aftercare program was to reduce post-release delinquency and drug use by: supervising youth's reentry into the community; assisting them in dealing with their families and other community institutions; and helping them to become engaged in appropriate educational or vocational efforts. In this section, we look at how well these objectives were achieved.

Arrests

Arrests or convictions have been the most widely used measures of recidivism. Although they reflect only a small portion of an offender's total criminal behavior, their advantage is that they are easily measured and do not require the active cooperation of the subjects.

Juvenile and adult court records in each site were reviewed to determine the number of arrests experienced by each of the participants during the first 12 months after their release, the seriousness of the charges, and their eventual disposition. The results are summarized in Table 4.1 and reveal no significant differences in the likelihood of arrest, conviction, or seriousness of the charges between the experimental and control groups in their respective sites. In Detroit, there was little difference between the groups of even a nonsignificant nature. In Pittsburgh, a smaller proportion of the experimental group were arrested or convicted for crimes against persons but the differences were still not significant.

Looking at the rate of arrests among those who experienced at least one arrest, we found little difference between groups in Detroit (1.6 for the controls versus 1.3 for the experimentals) and a small but nonsignificant difference in favor of the experimental group in Pittsburgh (2.9 versus 2.0).[1] A Kaplan-Meier survival analysis revealed no significant differences in time-to-first-arrest, although the experimentals appeared to fail a little sooner.

Thus, the post-release arrest data lend little support to the contention that the experimental programs reduced the frequency or delayed the timing of subsequent criminal behavior.

---

[1]With a larger sample size these differences might have been significant.

Table 4.1

Official Recidivism
(in percent)

| | Detroit | |
	Control (n=49)	Experimental (n=50)
Any arrest	18.4	22.0
Any conviction	14.3	14.0
Any arrest by type		
Person	6.1	6.0
Property	8.2	4.0
Drugs	2.0	8.0
Other[a]	2.0	4.0
Rate of arrests[b]	1.6	1.3
	Pittsburgh	
	Control (n=41)	Experimental (n=46)
Any arrest	48.8	47.8
Any conviction	46.4	34.8
Any arrest by type		
Person	17.1	8.7
Property	21.9	23.9
Drugs	7.3	10.9
Other[a]	2.4	2.2
Rate of arrests[b]	2.9	2.0

[a]Other offenses include probation violations and minor offenses.
[b]The rate is computed as the average number of arrests for active offenders.

Self-Reported Delinquency

Since only about 1 out of 20 offenses results in any arrest (Greenwood and Turner, 1987a; Blumstein et al., 1986), arrest data provide a somewhat limited view of an individual's post-release criminality. An alternative or complementary source for such information is the subjects themselves. Studies have shown self-reported data to be a fairly reliable source of information for the more serious forms of criminal behavior (Hindelang et al., 1981; Elliott et al., 1985).

In this evaluation, a modified version of the instrument developed by Elliott et al. (1985) for the National Youth Survey (NYS) was used to collect self-reported offense data for the years preceding placement and following release from residential custody (see Appendix B for a description of the instrument and scales). We also modified the scales developed by Elliott et al. (1985) to be parallel to the classification used for the official record data.

Self-reported prevalence rates (any participation) for various categories of offenses, for the years preceding and following the residential placement, and the percentage difference are shown in Tables 4.2a and 4.2b (see Tables A.9 and A.10 for complete data). In both sites, there was a reduction in almost all types of crime for both groups, but no significant difference between experimental and control groups. In Detroit, there was a greater reduction in self-reported general delinquency by the experimental group, in comparison to the controls. In Pittsburgh, there was less of a reduction reported by the experimental group compared to the controls. For example, the post-release prevalence rates were higher for index offenses, crimes against persons, and drug sales among the experimental group. But even these differences are not statistically significant, and they run counter to the finding that a smaller percentage of the experimental youth in Pittsburgh were arrested for violent offenses, shown in Table 4.1.

The frequency of self-reported delinquency, as measured by the annual offense rates, presents a different picture (see Tables A.11 and A.12). The median rates for active offenders were generally lower for the control group than the experimental group in Detroit. In Pittsburgh, however, the experimental group consistently reported fewer offenses.

In summary, post-release arrest records offer little support for even modest positive effects of the intervention on criminal behavior. Self-reported data for the Pittsburgh samples suggest a higher prevalence rate among the experimentals, but lower rates of offending, compared to the controls. However, none of these differences are statistically significant.

Self-Reported Drug Use

Since there is a strong relationship between drug use and continued criminality, (Elliott et al., 1985; Johnson et al., 1991), both residential programs put a heavy emphasis on substance abuse education and counseling and the aftercare workers were supposed to reinforce these efforts. As might be expected in a sample of youth like those in this study, before residential placement the prevalence rates for substance use were quite high. For example, more than 85 percent reported using any substance during the year preceding their placement (see Tables 4.3a and 4.3b), particularly alcohol and marijuana. About 28 percent of the Pittsburgh sample reported past year's use of cocaine and

Table 4.2a

Self-Reported Delinquency Prevalence Rates at Pre-Release and Follow-Up in Detroit, Michigan
(in percent)

	Pre-Release	Follow-Up	Percent Change
Control (n=22)			
General[a]	100.0	72.7	−27.3
Index[b]	95.4	27.3	−71.4
Person	95.4	31.8	−66.7
Property	90.9	27.3	−70.0
Drug sales	77.3	31.8	−58.9
Experimental (n=29)			
General[a]	100.0	48.3	−51.7
Index[b]	96.6	27.6	−71.4
Person	96.6	31.0	−67.9
Property	96.6	34.5	−64.3
Drug sales	89.7	27.6	−69.2

[a]General delinquency includes all offenses except status offenses (runaway and skipping school).

[b]Our modification of Elliott's definition of index offenses includes all UCR Part I offenses (assault, rape, robbery, burglary, theft, auto theft, and arson) and does not include gang fighting.

Table 4.2b

Self-Reported Delinquency Prevalence Rates at Pre-Release and Follow-Up in Pittsburgh, Pennsylvania
(in percent)

	Pre-Release	Follow-Up	Percent Change
Control (n=35)			
General[a]	100.0	77.1	−22.9
Index[b]	94.3	37.1	−60.6
Person	65.7	28.6	−56.5
Property	97.1	40.0	−58.8
Drug sales	68.6	34.3	−50.0
Experimental (n=38)			
General[a]	97.4	81.6	−16.2
Index[b]	92.1	42.1	−54.3
Person	71.0	44.7	−37.0
Property	92.1	42.1	−54.3
Drug sales	47.4	39.5	−16.7

[a]General delinquency includes all offenses except status offenses (runaway and skipping school).

[b]Our modification of Elliott's definition of index offenses includes all UCR Part I offenses (assault, rape, robbery, burglary, theft, auto theft, and arson) and does not include gang fighting.

6 percent reported using crack compared to about 6 percent and 9 percent, respectively, reporting such use in Detroit (see Tables A.3 and A.4).

The self-report data on post-release substance use and percentage change in the prevalence rates shown in Tables 4.3a and 4.3b show few minor differences in either site. In Detroit, there was a greater reduction in self-reported use of alcohol by the experimental group in comparison to the control group. In Pittsburgh, the experimental group reported lower rates of alcohol and hard drug use than the controls. Comparisons of average post-release frequency rates

Table 4.3a

**Self-Reported Drug Use Prevalence Rates at Pre-Release and
Follow-Up in Detroit, Michigan
(in percent reporting any use in the past year)**

	Pre-Release	Follow-Up	Percent Change
Control (n=22)			
Any substance	86.4	77.3	−10.5
Alcohol	72.7	77.3	+6.3
Marijuana	86.4	40.9	−52.7
Hard drugs	9.1	0.0	−100.0
Experimental (n=29)			
Any substance	96.6	75.9	−21.4
Alcohol	82.8	65.5	−20.9
Marijuana	86.2	44.8	−48.0
Hard drugs	17.2	3.4	−80.2

Table 4.3b

**Self-Reported Drug Use Prevalence Rates at Pre-Release and
Follow-Up in Pittsburgh, Pennsylvania
(in percent reporting any use in the past year)**

	Pre-Release	Follow-Up	Percent Change
Control (n=35)			
Any substance	100.0	82.9	−17.1
Alcohol	97.1	80.0	−17.6
Marijuana	91.2	42.9	−53.0
Hard drugs	42.9*	17.1	−60.1
Experimental (n=38)			
Any substance	97.4	71.0	−27.1
Alcohol	94.7	65.8	−30.5
Marijuana	76.3	47.4	−37.9
Hard drugs	21.1	7.9	−62.6

*Significant difference in pre-release time period between control and experimental group ($p < .05$) using a chi-square test of association.

of alcohol use between groups in Pittsburgh (see Table A.10) also show a decrease but nonsignificant difference in favor of the experimental group.[2]

Involvement with School or Work

According to self-reports of the youth at 12 months follow-up, there were no significant differences between groups in either site, in their rate of participation in school or work, as shown in Table 4.4. The majority reported that they were either enrolled in an educational program or working sometime during the 12 months following release from the residential placement. The rates of participation were fairly low in both sites, averaging between 8 and 18 weeks in school and 14 to 18 weeks of employment during the 12-month period. In Detroit, a significantly smaller proportion of the experimental youth reported participation in school or other educational programs. In Pittsburgh, more of the experimental youth were involved in school and work, but the difference (from the controls) was not statistically significant. Thus, despite the efforts of the aftercare workers to promote increased participation in legitimate activities, such as school and employment, there appears to have been little or no effect on the youth.

Involvement with Delinquent Peers

Most delinquency theorists would also agree that involvement with delinquent peers is a primary risk factor. In fact, admonitions to avoid bringing delinquents together in correctional programs constitute one of the few recommendations for reducing recidivism that some theorists have made (Elliott et al., 1989). We assessed the extent of exposure and commitment to delinquent peers using Elliott's NYS measures on both the pre-release and follow-up interviews. The data shown in Tables 4.5a and 4.5b show the changes over time in the reported behaviors of the friends of the sample youth[3] and the youth's commitment to delinquent peers.

In both sites, regardless of condition, youth reported a decrease in the number of friends involved in delinquent activities between the time prior to the current residential placement and the 12 months following placement. In Detroit, youth

---

[2]When we controlled on pre-commitment use rates, some of these differences became significant (for alcohol and hard drugs).

[3]Some youth claimed that they had no group of friends with whom they engaged in activities, so the sample size is reduced for some subgroups.

Table 4.4

Participation by Youth in School or Work During 12-Month Follow-Up

	Detroit	
	Control (n=22)	Experimental (n=29)
% in job/school[a,b]	90.9	79.3
% in school[a,b]	71.4	41.4*
Average number of weeks[c,d]	18.2	8.8
Average hours per week[c]	14.1	6.1
% in job[a]	63.6	67.9
Average number of weeks[c,d]	15.0	18.1
Average hours per week[c]	19.0	22.8

	Pittsburgh	
	Control (n=35)	Experimental (n=38)
% in job/school[a,b]	68.8	83.3
% in school[a,b]	45.7	56.8
Average number of weeks[c,d]	9.7	7.8
Average hours per week[c]	11.6	13.2
% in job[a]	45.2	51.4
Average number of weeks[c,d]	13.8	16.7
Average hours per week[c]	20.7	20.4

*Significant difference ($p < .05$) between control and experimental group using a chi–square test of association.

[a]These proportions are not adjusted for time at risk in the community.

[b]School participation is measured for all 12 months in the year and does not take into account the summer vacation.

[c]These rates were calculated for all youth and include zeroes, e.g., those who were not attending school or were not employed.

[d]The maximum number of weeks for either job or school was 52.

also reported a decrease in their commitment to delinquent peers. In neither site, however, did the aftercare program have a significant effect on the youth's associations with delinquent peers; both the experimental and control groups reported that fewer friends were involved in delinquent activities (see Table A.13).

Table 4.5a

Friends' Behaviors at Pre-Release and Follow-Up in Detroit, Michigan

Scale	Pre-Release Mean (s.d.)	Follow-Up Mean (s.d.)	Diff.
Control (n=22)			
Delinquent activities[a]	2.60 (0.81)	1.99 (0.79)	−.61*
Prosocial activities[b]	2.91 (0.72)	2.55 (0.70)	−.36
Commitment to delinquent peers[c]	2.12 (0.36)	1.88 (0.28)	−.24*
Experimental (n=29)			
Delinquent activities[a]	2.98 (0.66)	2.40 (1.07)	−.58*
Prosocial activities[b]	2.92 (0.92)	2.94 (0.77)	−.02
Commitment to delinquent peers[c]	2.16 (0.38)	2.02 (0.42)	−.14*

*Significant difference ($p < .05$) between time 1 and time 2.
[a]Items answered on a Likert scale from (1) none of them to (5) all of them.
[b]Items answered on a Likert scale from (1) all of them to (5) none of them.
[c]Items answered on a scale of (1) yes, (2) don't know, (3) no.

Personal Goals, Self-Efficacy, and Coping Skills

Both of the residential programs from which the study samples were selected devoted considerable efforts to assisting the youth to develop prosocial goals, increasing their sense of self-efficacy (through group projects, physical challenges, counseling, etc.), and helping them to develop coping skills for dealing with the kinds of high-risk situations that are likely to get them into trouble (arguments, frustration, substance abuse, etc.). According to recent cognitive/behavioral theories of behavior change, changes in actual behavior should be preceded by changes in these areas (Bandura, 1977). One objective of the aftercare programs in monitoring the youth's behaviors and providing counseling was to maintain any progress made in these areas during the residential program. Aftercare workers acted as role models in promoting prosocial goals and teaching coping skills.

Table 4.5b

**Friends' Behaviors at Pre-Release and Follow-Up
in Pittsburgh, Pennsylvania**

Scale	Pre-Release Mean (s.d.)	Follow-Up Mean (s.d.)	Diff.
Control (n=27)			
Delinquent activities[a]	2.67 (0.76)	2.25 (0.75)	−.42*
Prosocial activities[b]	3.06 (0.80)	3.14 (0.75)	+.08
Commitment to delinquent peers[c, d]	2.02 (0.47)	1.84 (0.45)	−.18
Experimental (n=32)			
Delinquent activities[a]	2.82 (0.88)	2.30 (0.69)	−.52*
Prosocial activities[b]	2.63 (0.93)	2.97 (0.66)	+.34
Commitment to delinquent peers[c, d]	1.92 (0.38)	1.90 (0.54)	−.02

*Significant difference ($p < .05$) between time 1 and time 2.
[a]Items answered on a Likert scale from (1) none of them to (5) all of them.
[b]Items answered on a Likert scale from (1) all of them to (5) none of them.
[c]Items answered on a scale of (1) yes, (2) don't know, (3) no.
[d]Sample size is 32 for controls and 36 for experimentals.

Our questions about personal goals included such items as the importance of: having money, friends, or self-respect; staying off drugs and staying out of jail, etc. (see Table A.14 for the complete set of items). In comparing the responses from the pre-release and follow-up interviews (using repeated measures ANOVAs), the general pattern we found was a drop in importance, away from prosocial goals (see Tables 4.6a and 4.6b). We did not find any significant differences between groups in Michigan. In Pittsburgh, we did find a significant interaction effect of time by experimental condition, with youth in the control group not exhibiting the general pattern of decline. When looking at the larger sample of 73 with follow-up data (see Table A.14), we did find some significant differences on individual items. For example, the experimental youth in Pittsburgh were more likely to value "keeping their life under control," "staying off drugs and alcohol," and "getting exercise" than the control group and placed less importance on marriage.

Table 4.6a

Changes in Attitudes and Behaviors in Detroit, Michigan

Scale	Pre-Release Mean (s.d.)	Follow-Up Mean (s.d.)	Diff.
Control (n=22)			
Personal goals[a]	4.45 (0.24)	4.09 (0.44)	−.36*
Self-efficacy[b]	4.76 (0.27)	3.99 (0.24)	−.77*
Coping skills[c]	2.91 (0.25)	2.44 (0.41)	−.57*
Experimental (n=29)			
Personal goals[a]	4.40 (0.24)	4.16 (0.40)	−.24*
Self-efficacy[b]	4.79 (0.56)	4.28 (0.42)	−.51*
Coping skills[c]	2.83 (0.25)	2.52 (0.32)	−.31*

*Significant difference ($p < .05$) between time 1 and time 2.

[a]All items answered on a Likert scale from (1) not at all important to (5) very important.

[b]All items answered on a Likert scale from (1) much worse to (5) much better.

[c]The categorical responses on this scale were rescored to (1) negative response, (2) neutral, (3) positive response, (4) positive action.

Our self-efficacy measures included self-assessments of changes in the youth's ability to stay out of jail, control his temper, avoid old friends, stay off drugs, etc.[4] As shown in Tables 4.6a and 4.6b, there was a significant difference over time in both sites, indicating a decay in self-efficacy. The data at follow-up alone, with the larger sample size in Pittsburgh, showed significant differences between the experimental and control groups (see Table A.15). The experimental youth in Detroit gave more support to the belief that they could keep their lives under control, make good lives for themselves, and stay out of jail, and overall they felt they had changed for the better. The experimental youth in Pittsburgh believed they were better able to abstain from alcohol and drugs.

---

[4]Youth were asked to compare the two time periods and indicate whether things were much worse or much better than before. For the pre-release interview, the comparison was between the time period before placement and the current time before release from placement. For the follow-up interview the comparison was between the time period before placement and the 12-month follow-up period.

Table 4.6b

Changes in Attitudes and Behaviors in Pittsburgh, Pennsylvania

Scale	Pre-Release Mean (s.d.)	Follow-Up Mean (s.d.)	Diff.
Control (n=23)			
Personal goals[a]	4.15 (0.25)	4.17 (0.34)	+.02**
Self-efficacy[b]	4.49 (0.35)	3.83 (0.51)	−.66*
Coping skills[c]	2.46 (0.42)	2.25 (0.56)	−.21
Experimental (n=33)			
Personal goals[a]	4.32 (0.34)	4.11 (0.30)	−.21**
Self-efficacy[b]	4.60 (0.33)	3.95 (0.46)	−.65*
Coping skills[c]	2.49 (0.34)	2.47 (0.30)	−.02

*Significant difference (p < .05) between time 1 and time 2.
**Significant difference (p <.05) for interaction effect of time by condition.
[a]All items answered on a Likert scale from (1) not at all important to (5) very important.
[b]All items answered on a Likert scale from (1) much worse to (5) much better.
[c]The categorical responses on this scale were rescored to (1) negative response, (2) neutral, (3) positive response, (4) positive action.

The coping skills questions required choosing among several possible responses to hypothetical situations such as: someone cutting in line; being falsely accused by a boss; or being at a party where people were using drugs. On these items there was some decay over time in Detroit, but none in Pittsburgh. On some of the individual items and the overall scale score, we found significant differences for the follow-up interview with the larger sample in Pittsburgh (see Table A.17). The experimental youth appeared better prepared to control their use of alcohol or drugs and to make better decisions in high-risk situations.

In summary, the intervention appears to have had slight but consistently positive effects on youth's personal goals, coping skills, and self-efficacy as measured at follow-up, although there was some decay from pre-release to follow-up. These effects were not large enough, however, to translate into significant changes in delinquent behavior or drug use. Whatever evidence we have in favor of modest improvements in the proportion of youth involved in delinquency and in rates of substance use is weak at best.

5. Conclusions and Recommendations

The implementation of the experimental programs did not proceed as smoothly as we had hoped. The flow of eligible youth into the experiment was slower than anticipated, causing staffing and cost overrun problems for the experimental program operators. The Michigan training schools did not release youth assigned to the experimental programs any sooner than the controls, increasing the overall cost of the experimental youth's placements. The Michigan program also lacked the power to apply appropriate sanctions against youth who failed to comply with the requirements of the program.

Data on the frequency of aftercare contacts suggest that the Pittsburgh program came much closer than the program in Detroit to our original model of tracking the youth several times a day. Nevertheless, both programs represent an order of magnitude increase in the level and intensity of contacts found in most juvenile parole programs, and both were regarded favorably by participating youth. In both sites, aftercare workers reported that they devoted considerable attention to getting the youth placed in suitable educational programs or jobs, and in working on their family problems. In both sites, youth in the experimental programs perceived them as more beneficial and rated their primary aftercare workers higher than those in the control groups.

In spite of these efforts, youth assigned to the experimental aftercare programs did not participate any more frequently in educational or work activities, compared to the controls, and were equally as involved as the controls in delinquent activities, drug use, and association with delinquent peers.

Both the experimental and control youth displayed a general pattern of decline in their sense of self-efficacy and prosocial goal orientation during their first year in the community. The experimental program in Pittsburgh appeared to slightly retard the rate of decay in all three areas, whereas the Detroit program appeared to retard the decline in self-efficacy but not the other two.

Although youth in the experimental programs in both sites rated the program and staff more highly than did youth in the control group, the increased frequency of contacts and services (including counseling and job advocacy) were not predictive of outcome, e.g., rearrest, recidivism, or relapse to drug use. The differences in attitudes and goal orientation and associations with peers were also not predictive of recidivism.

How do we explain the failure of the aftercare programs to have more of an effect on their subjects? There are a number of ways in which the programs could fail. One possibility is that the aftercare workers might not have been particularly effective at assessing the progress and problems of their clients. After all, predictions of risk based on clinical observations are notoriously inaccurate (Gottfredson, 1987). If this is the case, then the aftercare workers may have been able to provide only general support and assistance, rather than targeting specific problems or issues that were contributing to risk, and there might be a need for more formal methods of ongoing needs and progress assessment, including drug testing, reports by third parties, or tests of specific skills. However, the Sontheimer et al. (1990) evaluation discussed below suggests that aftercare workers can discriminate to some degree between those who are making good progress and those who are not.

It may be that changes in behavior or attitude occurred so swiftly that the aftercare workers did not have time to take corrective action, or that the aftercare workers may not have been effective in intervening in those instances and areas where slippages were observed to occur. Even with the intensive levels of supervision provided by the experimental program caseworkers, their amount of contact and degree of influence may have been fairly weak at best.

One explanation that always comes up when a new program is being evaluated involves the learning curve. Perhaps the programs were not as effective with the first group of youth they handled because the staff were still learning their functions. That explanation would have more credibility if we observed more differences in outcome between the two experimental programs, since the program in Pittsburgh appeared to encounter fewer management and staffing problems.

The explanation for lack of effect offered by officials with one of the program providers was the insurmountable nature of the problems and temptations encountered by the youth in their home communities, particularly the involvement of family members and friends in drug use, and the opportunities to become drug dealers themselves. By all accounts, the level of violence and drug trafficking in these communities has escalated considerably over the last few years.

It may be that the surveillance and casework model was simply inappropriate for the situations that these young men face. By all accounts, it was a real struggle to find jobs for these youth, and then often they would not keep them for more than a few days. Moreover, most of the families saw the problem (of delinquency) as primarily the youth's to deal with and were not interested in making major changes.

It may be that the resources devoted to the aftercare effort would have been better spent providing youth with more explicit educational and training efforts, using the cognitive-behavioral techniques that recent meta-analyses appear to have demonstrated are more effective (Andrews et al., 1990; Lipsey, 1991). If it is still believed that youth are less likely to recidivate if they are involved in productive educational or work activities, aftercare resources could be devoted to training youth in how to find and hold such positions, rather than helping them to find them directly. An alternative approach would be to require each youth to participate in some type of community-based program that targets an issue that might still be a particular problem after his release, such as substance abuse treatment/counseling or anger management. In either case, the focus would be on additional programming rather than surveillance and advocacy.

One problem with this approach would be getting the youth to participate, particularly those who need the most help. Recent experience with a number of drug court programs suggests that continued involvement in treatment, for high-risk individuals, can be enhanced by the use of behavioral contracts, which provide for significant rewards for complying with program requirements and penalties for violations. It might be that a similar form of "aftercare court," in which all transitional youth in a given area are required to participate bi-monthly, would be more effective in shaping behavior than the model tested in this study.

So what about the role of aftercare in juvenile corrections? Does it have a place? The answer to that question appears to depend on what we want aftercare to do and the seriousness of offenses committed by the youth involved. As a supplement to existing residential placements, the kind of aftercare program tested in this experiment does not appear to have much value. The $30 a day or $5,500 it requires to keep a youth in the program for six months does not appear to have any significant payoffs in improved public safety or benefits for the youth. However, as a substitute for time in residential confinement, for low-risk youth, intensive aftercare may be quite cost-effective, even if it does not reduce recidivism rates.

According to our data, only 22 percent of the Detroit youth in the experimental group were rearrested and only 28 percent reported committing a felony index offense[1] in the first year following their release. Among those who did commit index offenses, the median reported rate was approximately three crimes per year. If the length of residential commitment could be reduced without increasing the recidivism or offense rates, then these figures suggest that the average risk to the public represented by the early release of one of these youth would be less than one felony index crime per year.[2] As long as a youth can participate in the same kind of programming in the community that he does while in custody, it seems that intensive aftercare or intensive supervision is a worthwhile substitute for residential treatment. This is the same conclusion that Barton and Butts (1991) arrived at after evaluating the effectiveness of three different community supervision programs run by private providers for the Michigan DSS during the period 1983–1985, and finding no differences in recidivism between the community-based and institutional programs. The daily cost for the community-based programs was about one-third that of residential placement.

However, the picture is less clear with a higher-risk population such as that found in Pittsburgh, where about 48 percent were rearrested during their first year back on the street, and about 40 percent reported committing a felony index offense. Although the active offenders in the experimental group reported a median felony index commission rate of only three crimes per year, the control group actives reported a median felony index commission rate of 102. The median crime rate for the two groups is about 22 index felonies per year. For this group, early release may represent more of a risk than many communities are willing to tolerate.

A somewhat different strategy of aftercare supervision that involved a more proactive response to youth who showed signs of failure was found to have reduced the number of arrests experienced by similar high-risk youth by almost 50 percent (Sontheimer et al., 1990). The experimental study involved serious delinquents who had been committed to a residential facility (the Bensalem Youth Development Center) by the Philadelphia Juvenile Court. These youth were quite similar to our sample in Pittsburgh. Although the level of contact between the Philadelphia probation officers and the experimental youth was considerably less than in Pittsburgh, averaging only about 17 face-to-face contacts over six months, the Philadelphia officers still devoted most of their

---

[1] The definition of a felony index offense includes all part I UCR offenses (assault, rape, robbery, burglary, theft, auto theft, and arson) and does not include gang fighting as in Elliott's definition.

[2] Since youth in Detroit were not released early, which was the experimental design, we can use the available data only to infer average risk.

efforts to monitoring the youth and helping them establish appropriate contacts in the community.

Where the Philadelphia and Pittsburgh programs differed was in the aftercare workers' response to signs of failure. In the Philadelphia program, the aftercare workers were quicker to initiate revocation procedures against those youth who were not meeting the terms of their parole and immediate confinement for those charged with new offenses. However, the rapid response of the Philadelphia aftercare workers was found to be based on a selective rather than blanket policy. Apparently, the frequency of contacts they had with clients was sufficient to allow them to distinguish to some degree between those who were in need of confinement and those who were not. The end result of this policy was that recidivists and probation violators among the experimental group were more likely to be returned to custody than the controls, allowing fewer opportunities for multiple arrests. If the recidivists in our Pittsburgh experimental group had all been placed in custody immediately following their first arrest, it would have reduced the overall number of arrests by half.[3]

When synthesized with the results of other recent studies, the findings from this evaluation suggest alternative ways that aftercare programs might be structured. For lower-risk youth, intensive aftercare or community supervision might provide a cost-effective alternative to residential placement. However, rather than expending significant efforts on advocacy and social services, the Andrews et al. (1990) meta-analysis and this study suggest that aftercare efforts might be better focused on changing attitudes and behavior more directly related to delinquent behavior.

For more serious youth offenders, such as those in our Pittsburgh sample, the results of the Philadelphia aftercare evaluation and this study suggest that a quick custodial response to negative behavior might be considerably more effective than well-intentioned counseling and assistance in reducing subsequent arrests.

---

[3]Of the 46 youth in the VisionQuest experimental program, only four were returned to the residential group home for time periods from one to five days for problem behavior. Two youth were recommitted by the court to serve another residential stay with VQ after they committed new offenses. Because so few were returned to the program and we had limited information on the length of stay, we did not assess the effect of this return procedure on the final outcomes.

Appendix

A. Reference Tables

Table A.1

Background Characteristics of Sample in Detroit, Michigan

	Control (47)	Experimental (50)	Total (97)
Race			
Anglo	12.7	8.0	10.3
Black	87.2	90.0	88.7
Other	0.0	2.0	1.0
Family members in household			
Father only	2.1	2.0	2.1
Mother only	59.6	56.0	57.7
Both parents	19.2	22.0	20.6
Neither parent	19.2	20.0	19.6
Parents married and together	10.9	8.0	9.4
Family income from employment	34.9	25.0	29.7
Grades completed	8.1	7.8	8.0
Disciplinary problem	86.7	77.8	81.8
Learning disability[a]	43.5	43.5	43.5
Age			
At first arrest	14.4	14.4	14.4
At first adjudication	14.6	14.8	14.6
At current placement	16.2	16.0	16.1
Prior record			
No. of arrests	3.0	2.5	2.8
No. of adjudications	1.9	1.6	1.8
No. of probation terms	1.3	0.9	1.1
No. of placements	0.9	0.9	0.9
Current offense			
Person	55.3	51.0	53.1
Property	25.5	34.7	30.2
Drugs	10.6	10.2	10.4
Other	8.5	4.1	6.2
Gang member	29.8	24.0	26.8
Drug dealer	56.5	54.0	55.2
Drug use problem	46.8	48.0	47.4
Poly drug use	19.2	28.0	23.7

[a]Includes emotional disabilities.

Table A.2

Background Characteristics of Sample in Pittsburgh, Pennsylvania

	Control (40)	Experimental (46)	Total (86)
Race			
Anglo	17.5	13.0	15.1
Black	77.5	85.8	81.4
Other	5.0	2.2	3.5
Family members in household			
Father only	0.0	6.5	3.5
Mother only	62.5	54.5	58.1
Both parents	27.5	21.7	24.4
Neither parent	10.0	17.4	14.0
Parents married and together	8.1	2.2	4.9
Family income from employment	32.4	39.0	36.0
Grades completed	8.7	8.7	8.7
Disciplinary problem	83.9	94.6	89.7
Learning disability[a]	46.0	37.8	41.5
Age			
At first arrest	13.5	14.0	13.8
At first adjudication	13.7	14.4	14.1
At current placement	16.5	16.5	16.5
Prior record			
No. of arrests	4.8	4.6	4.7
No. of adjudications	3.5	3.7	3.6
No. of probation terms	1.6	1.4	1.5
No. of placements	1.9	1.9	1.9
Current offense			
Person	25.0	26.7	25.9
Property	60.0	46.7	52.9
Drugs	5.0	11.1	8.2
Other	10.0	15.6	12.9
Gang member	10.0	8.7	9.3
Drug dealer	12.8	9.1	10.8
Drug use problem	52.5	43.5	47.7
Poly drug use	25.0	26.1	25.6

[a]Includes emotional disabilities.

Table A.3

**Self-Reported Delinquency and Drug Use by Experimental
Conditions in Detroit, Michigan
(Pre-Release Interview)**

	Control (47)		Experimental (49)		Total (96)	
	Ever in Past Year	Annual Rate[a]	Ever in Past Year	Annual Rate[a]	Ever in Past Year	Annual Rate[a]
Elliott scales						
Felony assault	91.5	149.2	81.6	132.7	86.5	140.8
Minor assault	70.2	119.6	71.4	173.6	70.8	146.8
Robbery	45.7	76.8	49.0	41.6	46.9	58.8
Felony theft	76.6	335.4	83.7	236.8	80.2	285.1
Minor theft	68.1	107.4	67.4	69.8	67.7	88.2
Property damage	70.2	32.6	69.4	76.7	69.8	55.1
Forgery, fraud	48.9	56.4	49.0	73.0	49.0	64.8
Illegal services	80.8	639.8	83.7	593.8	82.3	616.4
Public disorder	48.9	42.7	34.7	40.9	41.7	41.8
Status offenses	95.7	229.4	98.0	307.0	96.9	299.8
School delinquency	97.9	266.1	100.0	323.5	99.0	295.4
Home delinquency	76.6	62.0	69.4	74.8	72.9	68.5
RAND scales						
General delinquency	100.0	2013.1	100.0	1849.1	100.0	1929.4
Index offenses	97.9	367.2	91.8	249.8	94.8	307.3
Person offenses	97.9	345.6	93.9	347.3	95.8	346.5
Property offenses	95.7	425.3	95.9	390.5	95.8	407.6
Drug sales	80.8	639.8	83.7	590.1	82.3	614.5
Substance use						
Alcohol	84.8	160.4	81.6	167.3	83.2	163.9
Marijuana	89.1	154.4	81.6	129.2	85.3	140.2
LSD	8.5	0.6	4.1	11.3	6.2	0.9
Heroin	0.0	0.0	2.0	0.0	1.0	0.0
Cocaine	8.5	22.3	4.1	18.8	6.2	20.5
Crack	10.6	27.7	8.2	18.9	9.4	23.2
Uppers	4.3	19.6	10.2	3.0	7.3	11.1
PCP	2.1	0.0	0.0	0.0	1.0	0.0
Methadone	0.0	0.0	0.0	0.0	0.0	0.0
Downers	0.0	0.0	2.0	0.0	1.0	0.0

[a]Annual rates were calculated as the total number of reported crimes in the category, divided by the number of days in a year.

Table A.4

Self-Reported Delinquency and Drug Use by Experimental Conditions in Pittsburgh, Pennsylvania
(Pre-Release Interview)

	Control (36)		Experimental (46)		Total (82)	
	Ever in Past Year	Annual Rate[a]	Ever in Past Year	Annual Rate[a]	Ever in Past Year	Annual Rate[a]
Elliott scales						
Felony assault	52.8	70.9	58.7	54.6	56.1	61.8
Minor assault	47.2	78.4	41.3	77.5	43.9	77.9
Robbery	22.2	25.3	30.4	35.1	26.8	30.8
Felony theft	91.7	306.5	89.1	496.8	90.2	413.2
Minor theft	75.0	77.5	69.6	224.9*	72.0	160.2
Property damage	50.0	10.0	45.6	50.5*	47.6	43.9
Forgery, fraud	36.1	31.8	34.8	53.9	35.4	44.2
Illegal services	66.7	441.0	52.2	246.4	58.5	331.9
Public disorder	55.6	37.9	32.6*	70.9	42.7	56.4
Status offenses	88.9	345.0	93.5	274.4	91.5	305.4
School delinquency	97.2	430.7	95.6	350.0	96.3	385.4
Home delinquency	22.2	1.6	45.6*	8.9	35.8	5.8
RAND scales						
General delinquency	100.0	1291.0	97.8	1523.8	98.8	1421.6
Index offenses	94.4	237.1	91.3	437.0	92.7	349.3
Person offenses	66.7	174.6	76.1	167.2	72.0	170.5
Property offenses	97.2	348.3	91.3	621.2	93.9	501.4
Drug sales	66.7	441.0	52.2	246.4	58.5	331.8
Substance use						
Alcohol	97.2	184.8	91.3	107.7	93.9	141.5
Marijuana	91.4	193.0	76.1	133.2	82.7	159.0
LSD	8.3	10.4	6.5	0.8	7.3	5.0
Heroin	2.8	0.0	4.4	0.0	3.7	0.0
Cocaine	41.7	59.2	17.4*	10.1	28.1	31.6
Crack	11.1	50.8	2.2	19.8	6.1	33.4
Uppers	11.1	1.8	8.7	28.3	9.8	16.6
PCP	5.6	0.1	4.4	0.0	4.9	0.1
Methadone	0.0	0.0	2.2	0.0	1.2	0.0
Downers	11.1	14.0	6.5	3.3	8.5	8.1

*Significant difference (at $p < .05$) between experimental and control groups using chi-square tests of association or t-test of means.

[a]Annual rates were calculated as the total number of reported crimes in the category, divided by the number of days in a year.

Table A.5

Analysis of Attrition Bias in Detroit, Michigan

| | Background | | | Follow-Up | | | | | |
| | Control | Experimental | Total | Control | | Experimental | | Total | |
				No Intvw	Intvw	No Intvw	Intvw	No Intvw	Intvw
Sample Size	47	50	97	24	22	22	29	46	51
% Nonwhite	87.2	92.0	89.7	79.2	95.4	95.4	89.7	87.0	92.2
% Drug users	46.8	18.0	47.4	58.3	31.8	40.9	55.2	50.0	45.1
% Person crime	55.3	54.0	53.1	37.5	77.3*	31.8	62.1*	34.8	68.6*
Age at first arrest	14.4	14.4	14.4	14.2	14.6	14.2	14.5	14.2	14.5
Number of prior arrests	3.0	2.5	2.8	3.4	2.2	2.4	2.6	2.9	2.6
Age at placement	16.2	16.0	16.1	16.0	16.3	16.0	16.0	16.0	16.1

*Significant difference ($p < .05$) between interviewed and noninterviewed groups using chi-square tests of association.

Table A.6

Analysis of Attrition Bias in Pittsburgh, Pennsylvania

	Background			Pre-Release							
	Control	Experimental	Total	Control			Experimental			Total	
				No Intvw	Intvw		No Intvw	Intvw		No Intvw	Intvw
Sample Size	40	46	86	16	24		5	41		21	65
% Nonwhite	82.5	88.0	84.9	87.5	79.2		60.0	90.2		81.0	86.2
% Drug users	52.5	43.5	47.7	50.0	54.2		60.0	41.5		52.4	46.2
% Person crime	25.0	26.7	25.9	31.2	20.8		60.0	48.8		23.8	26.2
Age at first arrest	13.5	14.0	13.8	13.7	14.1		13.7	14.1		13.4	13.9
Number of prior arrests	4.8	4.6	4.7	5.4	4.4		4.6	4.6		5.2	4.6
Age at placement	16.5	16.5	16.5	16.6	16.5		16.6	16.5		16.9	16.4

Table A.6—continued

| | Follow-Up | | | | | | Pre-Release and Follow-Up | | | | | |
| | Control | | Experimental | | Total | | Control | | Experimental | | Total | |
	No Intvw	Intvw	No Intvw	Intvw	No Intvw	Intvw	No Intvw	Intvw	No Intvw	Intvw	No Intvw	Intvw
Sample Size	5	35	8	38	13	73	17	23	13	33	30	56
% Nonwhite	100.0	80.0	87.5	86.8	92.3	83.6	88.2	78.3	76.9	90.9	83.3	85.7
% Drug users	40.0	54.3	75.0	36.8*	61.5	45.2	52.9	52.2	69.2	33.3*	60.0	41.1
% Person crime	20.0	25.7	25.0	26.3	23.1	26.0	35.3	17.4	16.5	30.3	26.7	25.0
Age at first arrest	14.0	13.4	13.6	14.1	13.8	13.8	13.5	13.5	13.6	14.2	13.6	13.9
Number of prior arrests	4.8	4.8	5.0	4.6	4.9	4.7	5.3	4.4	4.8	4.5	5.1	4.5
Age at placement	17.5	16.4*	16.8	16.5	17.1	16.4*	17.0	16.2*	16.7	16.5	16.9	16.3*

*Significant difference (p < .05) between interviewed and noninterviewed groups using chi-square tests of association.

Table A.7

Youth Perceptions of Aftercare Program
(At 12-Month Follow-Up)

	Detroit		Pittsburgh	
	Control (19)	Experimental (29)	Control (25)	Experimental (36)
Average months on aftercare	6.7	5.3*	4.6	5.8
The program helped me a lot[a]	2.7	1.6*	2.8	2.2
I got along with my worker[b]	2.0	1.5	2.2	1.4*
The staff seemed to care a lot about the kids[b]	1.7	1.6	3.1	1.9*
The program helped me stay out of trouble with the law[a]	2.3	1.7	3.0	2.2*
The program helped me get a job[a]	2.7	2.0	3.9	3.3
The program helped me stay in school	2.4	2.2	3.5	2.7
My experience in the program taught me how to get along with my family[a]	2.2	2.0	2.9	2.2
My experience helped me reenter the community[a]	2.7	1.8*	3.1	2.2*
My experience in the program helped me understand myself and my problems[a]	2.8	2.0*	3.0	2.1*
I am really glad I was selected for aftercare	2.7	2.3	2.7	2.2
I am proud that I completed the program	2.1	1.6	1.9	1.4
Scale score				
Program	2.6	1.9*	3.2	2.4*
Staff	1.8	1.6	2.6	1.6*

*Difference of means test significant at $p < .05$.

All items answered on scale of (1) strongly agree, (2) somewhat agree, (3) neither agree nor disagree, (4) somewhat disagree, (5) strongly disagree.

[a]Items included in program scale.

[b]Items included in staff scale.

Table A.8

Youth Perceptions of Primary Aftercare Worker
(At 12-Month Follow-Up)

	Detroit		Pittsburgh		
	Control (18)	Experi-mental (29)	Control (24)	Experi-mental (36)	
Friendly	1.6	1.3	2.3	1.3*	Unfriendly
Left me to myself[a]	2.9	3.4	2.7	3.6*	Always checking up on me
Spent a lot of time with me	2.9	2.2	3.5	2.0*	Spent very little time with me
I liked him/her a lot	2.1	2.0	2.5	1.5*	I disliked him/her a lot
Someone I could talk with	2.7	1.8*	3.0	1.9*	Someone I could not talk with
Took me out to (recreational) places	4.6	4.1	4.6	2.6*	Never took me any-where
Helped me get into school or voc training	3.3	2.6	3.8	2.5*	Did not help me with school or voc training
Helped me get a job	3.4	2.8	4.4	3.7	Did not help me get a job
Knew me well	3.1	2.0*	3.3	2.2*	Did not know me at all
Helped me get along with my family	3.0	2.5	3.7	2.2*	Did not help me get along with my family
Very helpful with my problems	3.1	2.1*	3.5	1.9*	Not at all helpful with my problems
Scale score	3.0	2.4*	3.4	2.2*	

*Difference of means test significant at $p < .05$.

All items answered on a Likert scale from 1 to 5, with 1 as left-column response, 5 as right-column response.

[a]The response on this item was reversed in calculating the scale score.

Table A.9

Self-Reported Delinquency and Drug Use by Experimental
Conditions in Detroit, Michigan
(During 12-Month Follow-Up)

	Control (22)		Experimental (29)		Combined (51)	
	Ever in Past Year	Annual Rate[a]	Ever in Past Year	Annual Rate[a]	Ever in Past Year	Annual Rate[a]
Elliott scales						
Felony assault	31.8	3.5	27.6	4.1	29.4	3.9
Minor assault	9.1	1.5	6.9	1.9	7.8	1.7
Robbery	9.1	0.1	13.8	0.6	11.8	0.4
Felony theft	18.2	48.3	24.1	2.6	21.6	22.3
Minor theft	9.1	0.5	17.2	0.8	13.7	0.7
Property damage	9.1	1.0	10.3	0.8	9.8	0.9
Forgery, fraud	13.6	0.7	20.7	57.1	17.6	32.8
Illegal services	36.4	116.3	27.6	121.0	31.4	119.0
Public disorder	31.8	8.8	10.3	0.2	19.6	3.9
Status offenses	13.6	6.6	13.8	6.1	13.7	6.3
School delinquency	13.6	7.3	10.3	6.0	11.8	6.6
Home delinquency	4.6	0.0	3.4	0.1	3.9	0.1
RAND scales						
General delinquency	72.7	208.0	48.3	211.6	58.8	210.1
Index offenses	27.3	42.4	27.6	4.1	27.4	20.6
Person offenses	31.8	5.2	31.0	6.6	31.4	6.0
Property offenses	27.3	50.0	34.5	60.4	31.4	56.0
Drug sales	31.8	74.9	27.6	121.0	29.4	101.1
Substance use						
Alcohol	77.3	41.1	65.5	65.8	70.6	55.2
Marijuana	40.9	47.8	44.8	48.3	43.1	48.1
LSD	0.0	0.0	3.4	4.5	2.0	2.6
Heroin	0.0	0.0	0.0	0.0	0.0	0.0
Cocaine	0.0	0.0	0.0	0.0	0.0	0.0
Crack	0.0	0.0	0.0	0.0	0.0	0.0
Uppers	0.0	0.0	0.0	0.0	0.0	0.0
PCP	0.0	0.0	0.0	0.0	0.0	0.0
Methadone	0.0	0.0	0.0	0.0	0.0	0.0
Downers	0.0	0.0	0.0	0.0	0.0	0.0

[a]Annual rates were calculated as the total number of reported crimes in the category divided by the time at risk in the community. Nonactive individuals (those who committed no crimes) are included in the calculation.

Table A.10

**Self-Reported Delinquency and Drug Use by Experimental
Conditions in Pittsburgh, Pennsylvania
(During 12-Month Follow-Up)**

	Control (35)		Experimental (38)		Combined (73)	
	Ever in Past Year	Annual Rate[a]	Ever in Past Year	Annual Rate[a]	Ever in Past Year	Annual Rate[a]
Elliott scales						
Felony assault	25.7	65.2	34.2	62.8	30.1	63.9
Minor assault	14.3	4.7	7.9	4.8	11.0	4.8
Robbery	2.9	10.4	10.5	2.0	6.8	6.0
Felony theft	31.4	180.4	39.5	36.6	35.6	105.6
Minor theft	28.6	85.8	26.3	16.6	27.4	49.8
Property damage	14.3	16.6	7.9	24.1	11.0	20.5
Forgery, fraud	22.9	46.2	13.2	4.4	17.8	24.4
Illegal services	37.1	303.6	39.5	300.0	38.4	301.7
Public disorder	37.1	72.5	26.3	52.7	31.5	62.2
Status offenses	31.4	32.5	26.3	60.9	28.8	47.3
School delinquency	31.4	44.4	26.3	75.7	28.8	60.9
Home delinquency	2.9	0.6	2.6	0.0	2.7	0.3
RAND scales						
General delinquency	77.1	1021.4	81.6	682.7	79.4	845.0
Index offenses	37.1	132.4	42.1	35.9	39.7	82.2
Person offenses	28.6	80.3	44.7	69.6	37.0	74.7
Property offenses	40.0	243.3	42.1	65.2	41.1	150.6
Drug sales	34.3	299.5	39.5	298.7	37.0	299.1
Substance use						
Alcohol	80.0	186.2	65.8	109.6	72.6	146.3
Marijuana	42.9	149.3	47.4	147.5	45.2	148.4
LSD	5.7	0.6	2.6	0.3	4.1	0.4
Heroin	2.9	0.1	0.0	0.0	1.4	0.1
Cocaine	5.7	26.7	5.3	27.5	5.5	27.1
Crack	11.4	52.8	2.6	0.3	6.8	25.5
Uppers	0.0	0.0	2.6	24.0	1.4	12.5
PCP	0.0	0.0	0.0	0.0	0.0	0.0
Methadone	0.0	0.0	0.0	0.0	0.0	0.0
Downers	0.0	0.0	0.0	0.0	0.0	0.0

[a]Annual rates were calculated as the total number of reported crimes in the category divided by the time at risk in the community. Nonactive individuals (those who committed no crimes) are included in the calculation.

Table A.11

Median Incidence Rates for Active[a] Offenders at Follow-Up in Detroit, Michigan

	Control		
	No.	Pre-Release	Follow-Up
General	16	1136	22
Index	6	27	2
Person	7	47	13
Property	6	53	6
Drug sales	7	387	153
	Experimental		
	No.	Pre-Release	Follow-Up
General	14	1420	147
Index	8	51	3
Person	9	72	12
Property	10	116	24
Drug sales	8	368	365

[a]Active offenders are defined as those who report committing the specific type of delinquent offense during the 12-month follow-up.

Table A.12

Median Incidence Rates for Active[a] Offenders at Follow-Up in Pittsburgh, Pennsylvania

	Control		
	No.	Pre-Release	Follow-Up
General	27	1038	234
Index	13	50	102
Person	10	54	133
Property	14	71	103
Drug sales	12	912	912
	Experimental		
	No.	Pre-Release	Follow-Up
General	31	489	102
Index	16	50	3
Person	17	25	11
Property	16	267	11
Drug sales	15	12	912

[a]Active offenders are defined as those who report committing the specific type of delinquent offense during the 12-month follow-up.

Table A.13

Behavior of Friends
(At 12-Month Follow-Up)

	Detroit		Pittsburgh	
	Control (22)	Experimental (29)	Control (27)	Experimental (34)
Attended school regularly?[b]	2.6	2.9	2.9	2.9
Damaged, destroyed, or marked up somebody else's property on purpose?[a]	2.2	2.1	1.8	2.0
Were involved in team or individual sports?[b]	1.8	2.7*	3.4	2.9
Smoked marijuana, pot, reefer, or hashish?[a]	2.6	3.0	3.1	3.4
Stole something worth between $1 and $50?[a]	1.7	2.3	2.0	1.9
Had steady jobs? (full or part time)[b]	3.1	3.3	3.3	3.3
Drank alcohol?[a]	3.5	3.4	3.7	3.4
Have gone into or tried to go into a building or vehicle to steal or damage something?[a]	1.4	1.8	1.9	1.7
Sold hard drugs such as cocaine, crack, heroin, PCP, and LSD?[a]	2.3	2.7	2.6	3.0
Stole something worth between $50 and $500?[a]	1.3	2.2*	2.0	1.7
Tried to get you to do something that was against the law?[a]	1.9	2.0	1.6	2.1
Used a weapon or force to make someone give money or things?[a]	1.6	2.2	1.6	1.6

Table A.13—continued

	Detroit		Pittsburgh	
	Control (22)	Experimental (29)	Control (27)	Experimental (34)
Shared their thoughts and feelings with you?[b]	2.7	2.8	2.8	3.0
Stole something worth more than $500?[a]	1.4	2.0	2.1	1.8
Hit or threatened to hit someone for no reason?[a]	2.3	2.6	2.2	2.4
Moved out of their parents' house?	2.8	2.6	2.7	2.8
Got hurt by someone else?	2.2	2.4	1.8	1.9
Were arrested?	2.6	2.8	2.7	3.2
Were committed to jail/prison or other placement?	2.2	1.9	2.4	2.6
Moved in with a girl?	2.0	2.4	2.5	2.6
Got a girl pregnant?	3.3	3.1	4.0	3.3
Scale score				
Delinquent activities[a]	2.0	2.5	2.2	2.3
Prosocial activities[b]	3.4	3.1	2.9	3.0

[*]Difference of means test significant at $p < .05$.

[a]These items included in scale score for exposure to delinquent peers: (1) none of them, (2) very few of them, (3) some of them, (4) most of them, (5) all of them.

[b]These items included in scale score for exposure to nondelinquent peers: (1) all of them, (2) most of them, (3) some of them, (4) very few of them, (5) none of them.

Table A.14

Personal Goals
(At 12-Month Follow-Up)

	Detroit		Pittsburgh	
	Control (22)	Experimental (29)	Control (35)	Experimental (38)
How important is:				
Getting a good job?	4.2	4.6	4.1	3.9
Getting a high school diploma or G.E.D.?	4.3	4.6	4.0	4.1
Getting along well with other people?	4.0	3.7	3.7	3.5
Succeeding at whatever you set out to do?	4.6	4.6	4.4	4.7
Being confident (sure of yourself) in certain situations?	4.6	4.7	4.4	4.5
Developing strong friendships?	3.8	3.8	3.6	3.7
Having money to buy clothes or records?	3.9	4.3	4.2	4.5
Getting along with your family?	4.7	4.6	4.6	4.6
Keeping your life under control?	4.7	4.9	4.5	4.8[*]
Being respected by others?	4.1	4.1	4.2	4.3
Not working too hard, but making enough money to get by?[a]	3.7	3.8	3.1	4.0[*]
Staying out of jail?	4.8	5.0	4.6	4.9
Having self-respect?	4.7	4.9	4.8	4.9
Getting a lot of money?	3.7	4.0	4.2	4.3

Table A.14—continued

	Detroit		Pittsburgh	
	Control (22)	Experimental (29)	Control (35)	Experimental (38)
Staying off of drugs and/or alcohol?	4.8	4.8	4.0	4.6*
Having sexual relationships?	4.0	4.0	4.3	4.4
Getting married some day?	2.8	2.5	3.2	2.1*
Having children of your own some day?	3.6	3.7	4.2	4.0
Doing a lot of exciting things?	4.0	4.0	4.1	4.4
Getting exercise?	3.9	3.9	3.4	4.1*
Scale score	4.1	4.2	4.1	4.1

*Difference of means test significant at $p < .05$.

All items answered on Likert scale of (1) not at all important, (2) not very important, (3) somewhat important, (4) pretty important, (5) very important.

[a]The score for this item was reversed when the scale was computed.

Table A.15

Self-Efficacy
(At 12-Month Follow-Up)

	Detroit		Pittsburgh	
	Control (22)	Experimental (29)	Control (35)	Experimental (38)
What kind of changes have there been during the past year in:				
Your relationship with your family?[a]	3.8	4.3	4.0	4.3
Your ability to get a job?[a]	3.8	3.9	3.7	3.6
Your ability to not commit crimes?[a]	4.1	4.8*	4.0	4.1
Your ability to get an education or job training?[a]	4.2	4.3	4.0	4.0
Your involvement in sports?	3.6	3.7	3.5	3.8
Your ability to control your temper?[a]	4.1	4.3	3.7	3.9
Your ability to stay out of jail?[a]	4.3	4.8*	3.9	4.0
Your ability to avoid some of your old (delinquent) friends?[a]	4.1	4.1	3.7	3.8
Your ability to get along well with other people?	4.3	4.6	4.0	4.1
Your ability to find a place to live and support yourself?	3.7	4.1	4.0	4.1
Your ability to abstain from drinking or doing drugs?	4.2	4.3	3.6	4.3*

Table A.15—continued

	Detroit		Pittsburgh	
	Control (22)	Experimental (29)	Control (35)	Experimental (38)
Your relationship with your girlfriend/wife?	3.9	3.9	4.0	4.1
Your ability to make a good life for yourself?	4.0	4.6*	4.2	4.3
Your ability to keep your life under control?	4.3	4.7	4.1	4.1
Your self-respect?	4.6	4.8	4.5	4.2
Your ability to have a lot of exciting and gratifying experiences?	4.2	4.1	4.1	4.1
Scale score	4.1	4.3*	3.9	4.0
Reduced scale score[a]	4.0	4.3*	3.8	3.9

*Difference of means test significant at $p < .05$.

All items answered on Likert Scale of (1) much worse, (2) worse, (3) about the same, (4) somewhat better, (5) much better.

[a]Reduced scale score uses items that are common to intake and follow-up interviews.

Table A.16

Coping Skills in Detroit, Michigan
(At 12-Month Follow-Up)

The following are descriptions of situations that you might face out in the community. Please tell me if you found yourself in one of these situations, what would you do?		Control (22)	Experimental (29)
If you were waiting in line for a movie and someone called you names for stepping on his shoe:	Scale	1.9	2.2
Would you		%	%
(1) swear back at him		22.7	14.3
(3) apologize, say I'm sorry		22.7	42.9
(2) just ignore him		45.4	35.7
(1) get in a fight		9.1	7.1
If your boss accused you of something you didn't do and tells you you are "fired":	Scale	2.8	2.7
Would you		%	%
(2) accept it		4.6	0.0
(3) try to explain the situation to him		72.7	65.5
(1) get angry and tell him off		9.1	13.8
(3) explain the situation to someone else		13.6	20.7
If you were hanging around with your friends and they asked you to help them beat up someone who had insulted them:	Scale	2.8	3.0
Would you		%	%
(2) go along with them, but not help		14.3	6.9
(3) say no, I don't want to fight		14.3	34.5
(4) try to stop them		47.6	41.4
(1) go along and help them		23.8	17.2
If you were at a party where many of the people were doing drugs, but you did not want to do drugs:	Scale	2.4	2.3
Would you		%	%
(3) leave the party		47.6	37.9
(2) stay, but not do drugs		47.6	48.3
(1) stay, and just smoke a little pot		4.8	10.3
(4) ask them to stop		0.0	3.4

56

Table A.16—continued

		Control (22)	Experimental (29)
If you were riding around with some friends and they stopped to buy liquor to drink in the car:			
	Scale	2.1	2.2*
Would you		%	%
(2) continue riding, but not drink		13.6	13.8
(3) ask to get dropped off		36.4	41.4
(2) offer to drive, but not drink		27.3	24.1
(1) continue riding and drinking with them		22.7	20.7
If you were on a break from your job and a co-worker lit up a "joint" and asked if you wanted to "get high":			
	Scale	2.2	2.3
Would you		%	%
(1) smoke the joint with him		13.6	20.7
(4) tell your boss		0.0	10.3
(3) say no		36.4	34.5
(2) go back to work		50.0	34.5
If you miss the bus or your car breaks down and you miss your appointment for a job interview and the employer says you can't come in for another one:			
	Scale	2.8	2.8
Would you		%	%
(3) ask him to give you another chance		19.1	14.3
(1) go out and get high or drunk		0.0	0.0
(3) try to explain why you missed it		57.1	67.9
(2) look for another job		23.8	17.9
Coping scale score		2.4	2.5

*Significant difference (p < .05) between experimental and control groups using t-tests of means.
Original categorical answers converted to scores of (1) negative, (2) neutral, (3) positive, (4) positive action.

Table A.17

Coping Skills in Pittsburgh, Pennsylvania
(At 12-Month Follow-Up)

The following are descriptions of situations that you might face out in the community. Please tell me if you found yourself in one of these situations, what would you do?		Control (35)	Experimental (38)
If you were waiting in line for a movie and someone called you names for stepping on his shoe:			
	Scale	1.7	2.0
Would you		%	%
(1) swear back at him		26.5	23.7
(3) apologize, say I'm sorry		26.5	36.8
(2) just ignore him		14.7	29.0
(1) get in a fight		32.4	10.5
If your boss accused you of something you didn't do and tells you you are "fired":			
	Scale	2.6	2.7
Would you		%	%
(2) accept it		5.7	5.3
(3) try to explain the situation to him		62.9	79.0
(1) get angry and tell him off		17.1	10.5
(3) explain the situation to someone else		14.3	5.3
If you were hanging around with your friends and they asked you to help them beat up someone who had insulted them:			
	Scale	2.7	2.7
Would you		%	%
(2) go along with them, but not help		5.7	24.3
(3) say no, I don't want to fight		37.1	16.2
(4) try to stop them		31.4	37.8
(1) go along and help them		25.7	21.6
If you were at a party where many of the people were doing drugs, but you did not want to do drugs:			
	Scale	1.9	2.3*
Would you		%	%
(3) leave the party		8.6	26.3*
(2) stay, but not do drugs		68.6	65.8
(1) stay, and just smoke a little pot		20.0	2.6
(4) ask them to stop		2.9	5.3

Table A.17—continued

		Control (35)	Experimental (38)
If you were riding around with some friends and they stopped to buy liquor to drink in the car:	Scale	1.8	2.2*
Would you		%	%
(2) continue riding, but not drink		5.7	5.3
(3) ask to get dropped off		17.1	44.7
(2) offer to drive, but not drink		42.9	29.0
(1) continue riding and drinking with them		34.3	21.1
If you were on a break from your job and a co-worker lit up a "joint" and asked if you wanted to "get high":	Scale	2.2	2.3
Would you		%	%
(1) smoke the joint with him		34.3	21.1*
(4) tell your boss		0.0	5.3
(3) say no		54.3	39.5
(2) go back to work		11.4	34.2
If you miss the bus or your car breaks down and you miss your appointment for a job interview and the employer says you can't come in for another one:	Scale	2.5	2.8*
Would you		%	%
(3) ask him to give you another chance		11.4	15.8
(1) go out and get high or drunk		5.7	0.0
(3) try to explain why you missed it		42.9	65.8
(2) look for another job		40.0	18.4
Coping scale score		2.2	2.4*

*Significant difference (p < .05) between experimental and control groups using t-tests of means.
Original categorical answers converted to scores of (1) negative, (2) neutral, (3) positive, (4) positive action.

B. Documentation of Random Assignment and Data-Collection Procedures

Random Assignment Procedure and Implementation

The random assignment procedure was designed so that program administrators at each site could develop the eligibility criteria for youth to be assigned to the aftercare program. Once eligible youth were identified, their names would be called in to RAND for the random assignment to the control or experimental group, based on a computer-generated randomized list. In Detroit, following assignment to the experimental group, the aftercare program worker would be notified by the program director and a contact would be made with the youth. In Pittsburgh, youth in the experimental group would be transferred by VisionQuest staff to a transitional group home.

In both Detroit and Pittsburgh, the major eligibility criterion was that the youth be returning to his family and reside within the city or county limits. Group leaders in the residential programs in Michigan and the regional treatment director for VisionQuest were responsible for identifying eligible youth for the intensive aftercare program and the RAND coordinator would call in the names for random assignment. In Detroit, some problems were experienced working with the DSS social workers responsible for the aftercare plans who were reluctant to refer youth to Diversified Youth Services. Although this did not affect the random assignment conditions for those in the experimental group, one or two of the youth who were assigned to the control group were placed in aftercare programs or halfway houses. In addition, there were some delays in the release of those youth in the experimental group because they did not leave the residential program until the peer group believed they were ready. The implementation of the random assignment in Pittsburgh was carried out smoothly, since the program was run by the same organization. There were some instances, however, in which experimental youth were terminated early from the program by the judge. In addition, some of the youth placed in the control group might have ended up in the intensive probation program.

In both sites, the case flow for random assignment was overestimated. Group leaders in Detroit were reluctant to nominate youth who had other aftercare plans. And in Pittsburgh the number of cases being processed by the juvenile court into VisionQuest was reduced. Although RAND extended the time period for the random assignment from the original 12 months to 18 months, the end result was a smaller sample than desired in Pittsburgh.

Informed Consent Procedure

As soon as youth had been assigned to the experimental or control program, RAND on-site field staff began data collection. Appointments were scheduled with the group leader to interview the youth. At the time of the interview, youth were given a description of the RAND evaluation, informed of the benefits and requirements of participation, and notified that all information would be confidential. If they agreed to participate in the RAND study, they were asked to sign the consent form. Signed consent forms were placed in the youth's files at the residential site and also forwarded to RAND.

Background Assessment Form

Official record information was coded from the individual files maintained by the residential program. The data collected included: demographics, family background, educational history, physical and mental health, drug use, and prior arrest record and previous out-of-home placements.

Pre-Release Youth Interview

Individual interviews that lasted approximately 45 minutes were scheduled with each youth in the experimental or control group and were conducted at the residential facility. Youth were paid $10 for their participation. The interview was primarily based on the National Youth Survey by Elliott et al. (1989) and covered a range of topics, including personal goals, self-efficacy, coping skills, exposure to delinquent and prosocial peers, self-reported drug use, and delinquency.

Calendar

The calendar was designed to capture information about the three years before the current residential placement. Information was coded from the background files and youth were asked to verify when they were at home and when they were in placements. Later in the interview the calendar was used in conjunction with the questions concerning behaviors during the past time period that they were at home.

Personal Goals

The 20 questions on personal goals asked for the youth's current perceptions of the importance of an activity. These activities included academic and employment success, self confidence, self-respect, relationships, and avoidance of drug use and delinquency. Each item was rated on a Likert scale from (1) very important to (5) not at all important. One item was reversed when the scaling was performed. A scale score was derived by taking the individual's mean score on all of the items. The reliability of the scale was tested independently for each site. Cronbach's alpha for the scale was .54 for Detroit and .75 for Pittsburgh.

Perception of Program

Nine questions asked about the youth's experience in the residential program. These questions were answered on a scale from (1) very true to (5) not true at all. The subset of items used in the Skillman evaluation was chosen to represent three areas: program helpfulness in terms of providing useful skills, program opportunity, and program fairness. The subsets of items for each of these three areas were scaled and the reliability was tested. Cronbach's alpha ranged from .64 to .72 in Detroit and averaged .74 in Pittsburgh for the three different scales.

Self-Reported Delinquency

Slight modifications were made to Elliott's self-report delinquency checklist from the National Youth Survey for its use in the present study. For example, the three specific items used to measure assault with identification of the type of victim (teacher, parent, other person) were combined into one item for assault on any victim. The same reduction process was used for questions on robbery and property damage.

For each of the 29 items in the final checklist, youth were asked to answer either with the exact number of times in the past year or according to a category, e.g., twice per week. Prevalence rates were calculated from the proportion of persons who either gave the exact number or a categorical response. Annual incidence or frequency rates were calculated by taking either the exact number of times reported for the past year or by using the median value for that category based on an annual rate of 365 days. For example, if the respondent reported stealing a car every two to three weeks in the past year, the median value would be 22 times per year.

For the analysis we used the 11 scales developed by Elliott et al. (1985), plus the two measures of school and home delinquency. We created five new scales for our analysis that are slight modifications of the general categories used by Elliott et al. General delinquency includes almost all of the items on the questionnaire, except for school and home delinquency items that are status offenses. Index offenses include all UCR Part I offenses—arson, assault, auto theft, burglary, rape, robbery, and theft. Person offenses include all minor and felony assaults—rape, robbery and gang fighting. Property offenses include minor and felony theft, property damage, burglary, forgery, and fraud. Drug sales includes selling of marijuana or hard drugs. Three measures were created for each scale and category, a prevalence rate, i.e., any delinquency in the past year, the actual incidence reported (number of times), and the annual delinquency rate, controlling for time at risk.

Self-Reported Drug Use

Elliott's self-report delinquency checklist was slightly modified for the present evaluation by expanding the specification of the types of drugs. Nine categories of drug or alcohol use were listed and crack cocaine use was listed separately from cocaine use. In addition, different categorical responses were used than in Elliott et al. (1989), allowing specification of greater frequency of use. In the analysis, the drug use questions were scored in the same manner as the delinquency items, either using the actual number of times or calculating the number based on the median value for a category. The same measures constructed for self-reported delinquency were also constructed for drug use, i.e., prevalence, incidence, and annual rate, controlling for time at risk.

Friends' Behavior

Three measures of friends' behavior were constructed, including Elliott's 11 items measuring "exposure to delinquent peers" and Elliott's three items measuring "commitment to delinquent peers." One item was added to Elliott's exposure to delinquent peers measure, reflecting association with more violent peers. Four additional questions were added to measure exposure to nondelinquent peers or association with peers involved in nondelinquent activities. Each of the questions for the exposure to delinquent and nondelinquent peers scales was answered on a Likert scale from (1) all of them to (5) none of them. Cronbach's alpha for the exposure to delinquent peers scale was high in both sites, about .89, and was slightly lower for the exposure to non-delinquent peers scale, .78. These two scales were kept separate because

Cronbach's alpha for the combined scale was low. Elliott's items measuring "commitment to delinquent peers" were not as reliable; Cronbach's alpha for this scale was about .57 in both sites.

Self-Efficacy and Motivation

Thirteen items measuring a youth's beliefs about future success in controlling his behavior were included in this section. These questions were composed by RAND staff members Peter Greenwood, Susan Turner, and Elizabeth Deschenes. They represent both the motivation to change and different dimensions of self-efficacy. Youth were asked to respond to the items in terms of whether they thought their chances for success were (1) much better, (2) somewhat better, (3) about the same, (4) somewhat worse, or (5) much worse than before the residential program. Since the items were rated on a Likert scale, a scale score was derived by taking the individual's mean score for the items he had answered. There was sufficient reliability in the reduced set of items common to both the pre-release and follow-up interviews, as well as in the complete set of items. Cronbach's alpha was .69 for Detroit and .81 for Pittsburgh.

Coping Skills

Eight questions were designed by Greenwood and Deschenes and modeled after items developed by Hays and Ellickson for Project Alert and coping mechanisms discussed by Bugen and Hawkins (1981). The Project Alert questions were designed to measure individual resistance self-efficacy in avoiding peer pressure to use drugs (Hays and Ellickson, 1990). The Coping Assessment Battery developed by Bugen and Hawkins identified 11 factors of how to deal with problems: decisionmaking, adult social support, cognitive coping, peer social support, substance use, physical exercise, aggression, social entertainment, individual relaxation, parental support, and prayer. The relapse prevention literature (Marlatt and Gordon, 1985) argues that persons can avoid relapse to drug use (or other behaviors) by developing coping mechanisms to deal with high-risk situations.

The questions used in the present study were designed to represent possible situations that youth would be facing as they reentered the community. Rather than use an open-ended format, the categorical responses were designed to measure youth's ability to "cope" with the situation and act in a socially appropriate manner as opposed to a socially inappropriate one. The items were rescaled and given values of 1 for an inappropriate response, 2 for a neutral or passive response (such as ignoring the situation), and 3 for an appropriate active response. For two of the items, the categorical response was given a weight of 4 for an active response that meant asking others to conform. These items were combined into a general scale of coping skills. Cronbach's alpha was .68 in Detroit and .83 in Pittsburgh.

Youth Needs Assessment

The 10 questions in this section were designed to measure whether the youth felt they had received help in these areas while in the residential program and whether they believed they would need help in these areas while they were in the community. Separate scales were derived to measure current needs and future needs. For current needs, a score of 1 represented that they did not need help, a score of 2 that they needed help and were getting it in the residential program, and a score of 3 that they needed help and were not getting it. An individual mean was computed to represent the average current needs. The items on future needs were scored either as no (0) or yes(1) and the scale derived by taking a simple sum across the items. Cronbach's alpha for the scale of current needs was .81 in Detroit and .71 in Pittsburgh.

Youth Three- and Six-Month Interviews

During the first year of follow-up data collection, youth were contacted at three and six months following release to the community to schedule follow-up interviews. Tracking youths at this point in time proved to be expensive and difficult and when the funding for the first two years ended and no further support was forthcoming for several months, the three- and six-month interviews were discontinued. It was possible to obtain some of the information that was gathered in the three- and six-month interviews at 12 months. However, in some cases when youth were uncooperative in the interview process, they were not asked to complete the three- and six-month interviews.

The three- and six-month interviews were designed to gather information on the type of services provided to the youth and their families. The interview items were identical and covered the last three-month period since release to the community (or the prior interview). Youth were asked to report the frequency of face-to-face or telephone contacts per month with their aftercare worker, social worker, or probation officer. They were also asked to report on the number of sessions in counseling (individual, peer, family, drug, or alcohol), the number of days in school or vocational training, and the number of days employed (part-time or full-time). In addition, youth were asked questions about their association with delinquent peers, their involvement in conventional activities, and how they felt about their progress on aftercare. Questions on self-reported delinquency and drug use were added to the six-month interview.

Youth Twelve-Month Interview

Approximately 12 months after youth's release from the residential program back to the community, RAND on-site staff attempted to locate each youth for an interview. Various tracking methods were used, including: searching the Department of Social Service and Juvenile Court records, contacting the social worker or probation officer, calling the family or other relative, checking the criss-cross directories, getting information from the post office, checking social welfare registers, and making a visit to the last known address to talk to neighbors.

The 12-month follow-up interview used many of the same measures as the pre-release (intake) interview and took about an hour to complete. Each youth was paid $20 upon completion of the interview. The major areas covered were: recent and current family living situation, school attendance and educational achievement, employment record, general and mental health, significant life events, self-reported delinquency and drug use, program and staff perception, coping skills, and self-efficacy.

Calendar

The calendar was designed to capture information about the 12 months in the community following a youth's release from residential placement. Youth were asked to report when they were at home and when they were in placements. There was no verification of youth's information with official records. Later in the interview, the calendar was used in conjunction with the questions concerning behaviors during the past 12 months to verify the time period during which they were at risk.

Personal Goals

The section on personal goals was exactly the same as was used in the pre-release interview. Cronbach's alpha for the follow-up interview on this scale was .87 in Detroit and .84 in Pittsburgh.

Experiences with Family, Job, and School

These questions were taken from the youth follow-up interview for the evaluation of the Paint Creek Youth Center (Greenwood and Turner, 1993). They were designed to measure the youth's adaptation back in his family, school, and job. Questions were also added to measure general physical and mental health, any illnesses or accidents, and critical events that may have affected the youth's behavior.

Self-Efficacy and Motivation

Sixteen items were designed to tap different dimensions of self-efficacy. Eight items that had been used in the pre-release interview were repeated. An additional eight items were included to measure changes in behavior during the past 12 months relating to experiences in the community and personal goals. As before, each item was rated on a scale from (1) much better to (5) much worse. Youth were asked to compare their experiences during the past year to their behavior before the residential program.

The eight items identical to the pre-release interview formed one scale (an individual mean was taken over all the items) and another scale was derived from the individual's mean for all 16 of the items. Cronbach's alpha for each of the scales was high, .77 and .88 in Detroit, .82 and .91 in Pittsburgh (with the higher alpha for the scale with 16 items), suggesting that the combined items could be used as a score for self-efficacy, or the scale with fewer items could be used if comparing the changes over time.

Friends' Behavior

The same items from the Pre-Release Interview were used to form the three scales of exposure to delinquent peers, exposure to nondelinquent peers, and commitment to delinquent peers. As before, Cronbach's alpha was highest for the exposure to delinquent peers measure, .95 in Detroit and .86 in Pittsburgh, and lowest for the commitment to delinquent peers measure, .47 in Detroit and .62 in Pittsburgh, and average for the exposure to nondelinquent peers measure, .74 in Detroit and .66 in Pittsburgh.

Self-Reported Delinquency

The same 29 items used in the Pre-Release Interview were used for the Follow-Up Interview. And the items were scaled in the same manner, creating three measures of self-reported delinquency: a prevalence rate, i.e., any delinquency in the past year, the actual incidence reported, and the delinquency rate, controlling for time at risk. One other question that was asked in this section was the number of days, weeks, or months between the time of release to the community and the first delinquent act. This question was recalculated to the number of days between release and first event for use in the survival analysis.

Self-Reported Drug Use

The same items that were used in the Pre-Release Interview were used for the Follow-Up Interview. One other question that was asked in this section was the number of days, weeks, or months between the time of release to the community and the first use of drugs or alcohol. This question was recalculated to the number of days between release and first event for use in the survival analysis.

Perception of Program and Staff

The eight items asked in the Pre-Release Interview about the residential program were repeated in the Follow-Up Interview to measure the same characteristics for the aftercare program. Another five items specifically about the aftercare program were also added. As before, youth were asked to rate the program on a Likert scale from (1) strongly agree to (5) strongly disagree. Two scales were derived, one measuring program perception, and the other rating all of the staff in the program. Cronbach's alpha for the program scales in Detroit was .94 for the program and .84 for the staff questions. For the Pittsburgh data, Cronbach's alpha was .94 for the program and .90 for the staff scale.

Eleven items, taken from the Violent Juvenile Offender study (Fagan, 1990), were used to measure the youth's perception of his primary aftercare worker. Youth were asked to rate the worker on each separate scale, for example, from very friendly to very cold. The items were chosen to represent the characteristics in a good aftercare worker. The full set of items was scaled, taking the individual mean. Cronbach's alpha of .87 in Detroit and .90 in Pittsburgh, showed that the scale was reliable.

Coping Skills

All but one of the items used in the Pre-Release Interview to measure coping skills were used in the Follow-Up Interview. The same scoring and scaling procedures were used. The Cronbach's alpha for the follow-up interview, .60 for Detroit and .76 for Pittsburgh, indicated sufficient reliability.

Caseworker Interviews

We had gathered information identifying the caseworker (private aftercare, social worker, or probation officer) for each youth assigned to the RAND evaluation before his release to the community. At three and six months following the release of each individual, the caseworker would be contacted and asked about the youth's progress. In general, it was easier to contact the workers in the private agencies providing aftercare, since there was less turnover of cases. In Detroit, many of the DSS social workers were reluctant to participate in the evaluation, some because they no longer had the individual on their caseload. In both sites, there was low response for cases in which the youth had already turned 18. In Pittsburgh, some of the youth were placed on intensive probation and the case changed hands. It proved difficult in both sites to reach the caseworkers of youth in the control group.

The three- and six-month interviews were designed to gather information on the type of services provided to the youth and their families. The interviews were identical and covered the last three-month period since release to the community (or the prior interview). The caseworkers were asked to report the frequency of face-to-face, telephone, and collateral contacts per month with the youth and his family. Staff were also asked to report the youth's involvement in counseling (individual, peer, family, drug, or alcohol), the number of days in school or vocational training, and the number of days employed (part-time or full-time). In addition, caseworkers were asked questions about the youth's association with delinquent peers, their involvement in conventional activities, signs of problems with their families or the police, the youth's delinquency and drug use, and their progress on aftercare.

Official Record Checks

Comparable, but different, sources of information were used to collect the official record follow-up data in the two sites. In Detroit, the Wayne County Department of Social Services files were checked for each youth from the time of release until the age of 18. The records at the Adult Recorders' Court for Wayne County were also checked. These court records keep track of only those cases that would have come before the court and would therefore not include arrests for which there was not enough evidence to prosecute. In Pittsburgh, two sources were checked for each individual, the Allegheny County Juvenile Court and the Allegheny County Adult Recorders' Court. Since the majority of youth turned 18 within a few months after their release from VisionQuest, there were few records in the Juvenile Court. In both Detroit and Pittsburgh, the records that were used were limited to arrests within the original county of jurisdiction; consequently, any arrests in nearby counties were missed.

For each arrest record found in the individual's file, data were coded on the date of the arrest, the type of charges filed, the date of the disposition, and the type of disposition. If the youth was adjudicated delinquent or found guilty, the types of conviction offenses, the date of the sentence, and the type of sentence were recorded. If the individual was sentenced to jail, prison, probation, or other facility, the dates of entry to and exit from the facility were recorded (if information was available).

Bibliography

Akers, Ronald L., *Deviant Behavior: A Social Learning Approach* (2nd ed.)., Wadsworth Press, Belmont, California, 1977.

Altschuler, David M., and Troy L. Armstrong, "Intensive Aftercare for the High-Risk Juvenile Parolee: Issues and Approaches in Reintegration and Community Supervision," in Troy L. Armstrong (ed.), *Intensive Interventions with High-Risk Youths: Promising Approaches in Juvenile Probation and Parole*, Willow Tree Press, Monsey, New York, 1991.

Andrews, D. A., Ivan Zinger, R. D. Hoge, James Bonta, Paul Gendreau, and Francis T. Cullen, "Does Correctional Treatment Work? A Clinically-Relevant and Psychologically-Informed Meta-Analysis," *Criminology*, Vol. 28, No. 3, pp. 369–404, 1990.

Bandura, Albert, *Social Learning Theory*, Prentice-Hall, Englewood Cliffs, New Jersey, 1977.

Barton, William H., and Jeffrey A. Butts, "Intensive Supervision Alternatives for Adjudicated Juveniles," in Troy L. Armstrong (ed.), *Intensive Interventions with High-Risk Youths: Promising Approaches in Juvenile Probation and Parole*, Willow Tree Press, Monsey, New York, 1991.

Blumstein, Alfred, Jacqueline Cohen, and Christy Visher (eds.), *Criminal Careers and Career Criminals*, Vol. I, National Research Council, National Academy Press, Washington, D.C., 1986.

Bugen, L. A., and R. C. Hawkins III, *The Coping Assessment Battery: Theoretical and Empirical Foundations*, paper presented at the American Psychology Association Meeting, Los Angeles, California, August 1981.

Cloward, Richard A., and Lloyd Ohlin, *Delinquency and Opportunity: A Theory of Delinquent Gangs*, Free Press, New York, New York, 1960.

Coates, Richard B., A. D. Miller, and Lloyd E. Ohlin, *Diversity in a Youth Correctional System: Handling Delinquents in Massachusetts*, Ballinger Press, Cambridge, Massachusetts, 1978.

Elliott, Delbert S., David Huizinga, and Scott Menard, *Multiple Problem Youth: Delinquency, Substance Use, and Mental Health Problems*, Springer-Verlag, New York, 1989.

Elliott, Delbert S., David Huizinga, and Suzanne S. Ageton, *Explaining Delinquency and Drug Use*, Sage Publications, Beverly Hills, California, 1985.

Fagan, Jeffrey A., "Treatment and Re-Integration of Violent Delinquents: Experimental Results," *Justice Quarterly*, Vol. 7, No. 2, pp. 233–263, 1990.

72

Farrington, David P., "Implications of Criminal Career Research for the Prevention of Offending," *Journal of Adolescence*, Vol. 13, pp. 93–113, 1990.

Gottfredson, Don M., "Prediction and Classification in Criminal Justice Decision Making," in Don M. Gottfredson and Michael Tonry (eds.), *Prediction and Classification: Criminal Justice Decision Making*, Vol. 9, University of Chicago Press, Chicago, Illinois, 1987.

Gottfredson, Michael R., and Travis Hirschi, *A General Theory of Crime*, Stanford University Press, Stanford, California, 1990.

Greenwood, Peter W., with Allan F. Abrahamse, *Selective Incapacitation*, RAND, R-2815-NIJ, August 1982.

Greenwood, Peter W., and Susan Turner, "Evaluation of the Paint Creek Youth Center: A Residential Program for Serious Delinquents," *Criminology*, Vol. 31, No. 2, pp. 263–279, May 1993.

Greenwood, Peter W., and Susan Turner, *Selective Incapacitation Revisited: Why the High-Rate Offenders Are Hard To Predict*, RAND, R-3397-NIJ, March 1987a.

Greenwood, Peter W., and Susan Turner, *The VisionQuest Program: An Evaluation*, RAND, R-3445-OJJDP, November 1987b.

Greenwood, Peter W., and Franklin E. Zimring, *One More Chance: The Pursuit of Promising Intervention Strategies for Chronic Juvenile Offenders*, RAND, R-3214-OJJDP, May 1985.

Hawkins, David J., Denise M. Lishner, Jeffrey M. Jenson, and Richard Catalano, "Delinquents & Drugs: What the Evidence Suggests about Prevention and Treatment Programming," in Barry S. Brown and Arnold R. Mills (eds.), *Youth at High Risk for Substance Abuse*, National Institute on Drug Abuse, DHHS Publication No. ADM 87-1537, 1987.

Hays, Ronald D., and Phyllis L. Ellickson, *How Generalizable Are Adolescent Beliefs About Pro-Drug Pressures and Resistance Self-Efficacy?* RAND, N-3108-CHF, February 1990.

Hindelang, Michael, Travis Hirschi, and Joseph Weis, *Measuring Delinquency*, Sage Publications, Beverly Hills, California, 1981.

Hirschi, Travis, *Causes of Delinquency*, University of California Press, Berkeley, California, 1969.

Huizinga, David, Rolf Loeber, and Terence Thornberry, *Urban Delinquency and Substance Abuse: Technical Reports*, Vols. I, II, and Appendices. Program of Research on the Causes and Correlates of Delinquency, Office of Juvenile Justice and Delinquency Prevention, U.S. Department of Justice, September 1991.

Johnson, Bruce, Eric D. Wish, James Schmeidler, et al., "Concentration of Delinquent Offending: Serious Drug Involvement and High Delinquency Rates," *Journal of Drug Issues*, Vol. 21, No. 2, pp. 205–229, 1991.

Lipsey, Mark W., "Juvenile Delinquency Treatment: A Meta-Analytic Inquiry into the Variability of Effects," in *Meta-Analysis for Explanation: A Casebook*, Russell Sage Foundation, New York, New York, 1991.

Loeber, Rolf, and Magda Stouthamer-Loeber, "Family Factors as Correlates and Predictors of Juvenile Conduct Problems and Delinquency," in Michael Tonry and Norval Morris (eds.), *Crime and Justice: An Annual Review of Research*, Vol. 7, University of Chicago Press, Chicago, Illinois, 1986.

Marlatt, G. Alan, and Judith R. Gordon, *Relapse Prevention: Maintenance Strategies in the Treatment of Addictive Behaviors*, The Guilford Press, New York, New York, 1985.

Merton, Robert K., *Social Theory and Social Structure*, Free Press, New York, New York, 1968.

Ohlin, Lloyd E., Robert B. Coates, and Alden D. Miller, *Reforming Juvenile Corrections: The Massachusetts Experience*, Ballinger Publishing Company, Cambridge, Massachusetts, 1978.

Reiss, Albert J., and Jeffrey A. Roth, *Understanding and Preventing Violence*, National Academy Press, Washington, D.C., 1993.

Sontheimer, Henry, Lynne Goodstein, and Michael Kovacevic, *Philadelphia Intensive Aftercare Probation Evaluation Project*, Pennsylvania Commission on Crime and Delinquency, Pennsylvania Juvenile Court Judges' Commission, Shippensburg University of Pennsylvania, Shippensburg, Pennsylvania, December 1990.

Thornberry, Terence P., Stewart E. Tolnay, Timothy J. Flanagan, and Patty Glynn, *Children in Custody, 1987: A Comparison of Public and Private Juvenile Custody Facilities*, University at Albany, Albany, New York, March 7, 1989.